James Seabright, Jenny Topper,
Sue Scott Davison and Lee Menzies present

# OUR BOYS

by Jonathan Lewis

Cian Barry
Jolyon Coy
Arthur Darvill
Laurence Fox
Matthew Lewis
Lewis Reeves

Director
David Grindley

| Designer | Lighting Designer | Sound Designer |
|---|---|---|
| Jonathan Fensom | Jason Taylor | Gregory Clarke |

| Dramaturg | Casting Director |
|---|---|
| Miranda Foster | Stephen Moore CDG |

First performance of this production at the Duchess Theatre, London on 26
September 2012.

First produced at the Cockpit Theatre by William Butler-Sloss, by arrangement
with Rubicon Theatre Company, on 13 May 1993. It was subsequently produced
in March 1995 at the Derby Playhouse in association with Incidental Theatre
and, presented by Rupert Gavin, transferred to the Donmar Warehouse, London
on 12 April 1995.

www.OurBoysThePlay.com

# OUR BOYS

by Jonathan Lewis

| | |
|---|---|
| **Keith** | Cian Barry |
| **POM** | Jolyon Coy |
| **Parry** | Arthur Darvill |
| **Joe** | Laurence Fox |
| **Mick** | Matthew Lewis |
| **Ian** | Lewis Reeves |

| | |
|---|---|
| **Director** | David Grindley |
| **Designer** | Jonathan Fensom |
| **Sound Design** | Gregory Clarke |
| **Lighting Design** | Jason Taylor |
| **Dramaturg** | Miranda Foster |
| **Casting Director** | Stephen Moore CDG |
| **Assistant Director** | Katherine Hare |

| | |
|---|---|
| **Company Stage Manager** | Paul Bouchier |
| **Deputy Stage Manager** | Briony Allen |
| **Acting ASM** | Matthew Forsythe |
| **Understudy** | Edward Grace |
| **Acting ASM** | Sam Nicholl |

| | |
|---|---|
| **Fight Director** | Tim Klotz |
| **Props Supervisor** | Jemma Gardner |
| **Wardrobe Supervisor** | Laura Rushton |
| **Dialect coach** | Majella Hurley |
| **Speech therapist** | Annie Morrison |

| | |
|---|---|
| **General Management** | Seabright Productions and Squaredeal Productions |
| **Production Management** | Patrick Molony and Kate West |
| **Marketing** | Will Maidwell, Elaine McGowan and Martin Gray (EMG) |

| | |
|---|---|
| **Press** | Anna Arthur and Andrew Greer |
| | (Arthur Leone PR) |
| **Promotions** | Chris McGill (Milktwosugars) |
| **Production consultant** | Gareth Johnson |
| **Production photography** | Geraint Lewis |
| **Publicity photography** | Eric Richmond |
| **Publicity design** | Snow Creative |
| **Set construction** | Visual Scene |
| **Lighting equipment** | White Light |
| **Sound equipment** | Stage Sound Services |
| **Audio describers** | VocalEyes |
| **Captioners** | StageText |

Stage One is proud to award a Start-Up Fund for New Producers to Sue Scott Davison for *Our Boys*. The Start-Up Fund is an investment scheme that aims to kick-start the careers of outstanding new commercial theatre producers by awarding them up to £50,000 investment into a West End or Commercial Touring Production. The Fund is supported by individuals, trusts and businesses that care about the future lifeblood of commercial theatre. For more information please visit www.stageone.uk.com

**Cian Barry** | Keith

Theatre includes: *The Rivals* (Southwark), *The Member Of The Wedding* (Young Vic), *One Flew Over The Cuckoo's Nest* (UK tour), *The Grand Concer* (Old Vic). Television includes: *New Tricks* (Wall to Wall), *Titanic* (Deep Indigo Productions), *Doctors* (BBC), *Shameless* (Channel 4), *Waking The Dead* (BBC), *The Bill* (Thames), *Man and Boy* (BBC). Film includes: *RPG* (dir. David Rebordao), *Downpour* (dir. Claire Dix), *Ghost Town* (dir. Todor Chapkanov), *Holy Water* (dir. Tom Reeve), *In The Spider's Web* (dir. Terry Winsor), *Incomplete* (dir. Yann Demange).

**Jolyon Coy** | Potential Officer Menzies (POM)

Theatre includes: *Posh* (Royal Court and Duke of York's), *Edward II* (Manchester Royal Exchange), *The Prince of Homburg* (Donmar), *All's Well That Ends Well* (National Theatre). Television includes: *Henry IV Parts 1 and 2*, *Pete vs Life*, *Doctors*, *The Friday Night Club*, *Casualty*, *The Revenge Files of Alistair Fury*, *My Hero*, *The Bill*. Film includes: *The Deep Blue Sea*. Radio includes: *Dance To The Music Of Time* (BBC Radio 4).

**Arthur Darvill** | Parry

Theatre includes: *Doctor Faustus* (Shakespeare's Globe), *Marine Parade* (Brighton Festival), *Swimming with Sharks* (Vaudeville), *White Rabbit Red Rabbit* (Gate), *Terre Haute* (Trafalgar Studios, Edinburgh Assembly Rooms and tour, *Evening Standard* Awards nomination for Best Newcomer) and *Stacy* (Arcola). Arthur is a founding member of Fuego's Men Theatre Company. Film includes: *Robin Hood* (dir. Ridley Scott), *Sex & Drugs & Rock & Roll* (dir. Mat Whitecross), *Pelican Blood* (dir: Karl Golden). Television includes: *Broadchurch*, *The Paradise*, *Doctor Who*, *Little Dorritt*, *He Kills Coppers* and *The Verdict*. Radio includes : *Burning Both Ends*, *Gulliver's Travels*. Theatre music credits include: *Been So Long* (Young Vic/Traverse), *The Frontline* (Shakespeare's Globe), *Stoopid Fucken Animals* (Traverse), *It's About Time* (Latitude), *Is Everyone Ok?* (Latitude, UK Tour).

**Laurence Fox** | Joe

Theatre includes: *Treats* (Garrick), *'Tis Pity She's A Whore* (Southwark), *Mrs Warren's Profession* (Strand). Television includes: *Lewis* (ITV, seven series), *Fast Freddie* (ITV), *Wired* (ITV), *A Room With A View* (RDF), *Miss Marple* (Granada), *Whatever Love Means* (Granada), *Egypt* (BBC), *Jericho*

(ITV), *Colditz* (Granada), *AD/BC: A Rock Opera* (BBC), *Island At War* (ITV), *Foyle's War* (ITV). Film includes: *W.E.* (dir. Madonna), *Blackwater Transit* (dir. Tony Kaye), *Elizabeth: The Golden Age* (dir. Shekhar Kapur), *Becoming Jane* (dir. Julian Jarrold), *Wasp* (dir. Woody Allen), *The Last Drop* (dir. Colin Teague), *South From Grenada* (dir. Fernando Colomo), *Deathwatch* (dir. Michael J Bassett), *Gosford Park* (dir. Robert Altman), *The Hole* (dir. Nick Hamm).

**Matthew Lewis** | Mick

Theatre includes: *The Verdict* (Theatre Royal Windsor and tour). Film includes: *Wasteland* (dir. Rowan Athale), *Harry Potter and the Deathly Hallows: Parts I and II*, *Harry Potter and the Half Blood Prince*, *Harry Potter and the Order of the Phoenix* (all dir. David Yates) *Harry Potter and the Goblet of Fire* (dir. Mike Newell), *Harry Potter and the Prisoner of Azkaban* (dir. Alfonso Cuaron), *Harry Potter and the Chamber of Secrets*, *Harry Potter and the Philosopher's Stone* (both dir. Chris Columbus), *The Sweet Shop* (dir. Ben Myers). Television includes: *The Syndicate* (BBC), *Some Kind Of Life* (Granada), *Dalziel and Pascoe* (BBC), *Tenant of Wildfell Hall* (BBC), *Sharpe* (BBC), *Where The Heart Is* (Yorkshire TV), *City Central* (BBC), *Heartbeat* (Yorkshire TV).

**Lewis Reeves** | Ian

Theatre includes: *Muscle* (Edinburgh Fringe), *Twelfth Night* (tour). Television includes: Lee Nelson's *Well Funny People* (BBC), *Ben and Lump* (Channel 4), *Doctors* (BBC), *Holby City* (BBC), *White Van Man* (ITV). Radio: *And Then We Came To The End* (BBC Cardiff).

**Matthew Forsythe** | Acting Assistant Stage Manager and Understudy for Keith, Ian and Mick

Theatre includes: *The Life Of Henry Fifth* (RSC), understudy for Ferras/Willoughby in *Sense and Sensibility* (Tour) and *The Hang of Gaol* (Rolling Sky Productions), *Chekhov Vaudevilles* and *If It's a Boy* (Brick by Brick), *Much Ado About Nothing* and multiple other productions (Drama Studio London). Film includes: *Just Keep Floating* and *Tolerance* (Magnus Ahlberg Productions).

**Edward Grace** | Understudy for Joe, Parry and POM

Theatre credits include: *Out of Order* (British Theatre Playhouse), *Bound* (Bear Trap), *Tall Poppies*, *That Dark Place*, *Safety* and *A Hole in the Fence* (Box Of Tricks), *Angela Unbound* (Second Skin), *No Gypsy*

*Child of Mine* (Hampstead), *Closer* (ADC Theatre), and *The Mousetrap* (West End). Film and Television includes: *Credence Like* (Hansen Entertainment), *Dirty Money* (Insight Films) and *The Academy* (Peter Hinton).

**Sam Nicholl** | Acting Assistant Stage Manager and Understudy for Joe, Parry, POM

Theatre includes: *Funny Peculiar* (UK Tour), *The Provoked Wife* (Greenwich Playhouse), *Romeo and Juliet* (Tour of Italy) and *Oliver Twist* (Giant Olive Theatre Co). Film and Television includes: *Wounded* (Winner: Best Film, Marbella International Film Festival 2011, Big View Media), *Doctors* (BBC), *A Pinch of Anger* (Sudden Productions) and *Light Years from Home* (Virgin Media).

**Jonathan Lewis** | Playwright

Jonathan Lewis is a writer and director for theatre and television. He wrote and directed the original productions of *Our Boys* at the Cockpit Theatre, Derby Playhouse and Donmar Warehouse between 1993 and 1995. It won a Writers' Guild award and Jonathan was nominated for the Lloyds Bank Playwright of the Year. Other credits include: *Breakfast with Jonny Wilkinson* (as director) and *All Mouth* (as writer and director), both at the Menier Chocolate Factory, and Pitch Perfect (Tristan Bates and Tabard theatres). His one-man show *I Found My Horn* was critically acclaimed when it opened in 2008 and subsequently toured the UK and further afield, including a run at Hampstead Theatre and the Laguna Beach Playhouse. Jonathan is also an actor and has appeared in numerous plays and television dramas including working at the National Theatre and in the West End, and on TV in *Soldier, Soldier*, *Silent Witness*, *London's Burning* and, most recently, *Endeavour*.

**David Grindley** | Director

Theatre credits include: *Enron* (Tokyo), *Copenhagen* (Sheffield), *The Misanthrope* (Stratford, Ontario), *Journey's End* (Duke of Yorks), *Jeffrey Bernard Is Unwell* (Tour), *Six Degrees of Separation* (Old Vic), *A Midsummer Night's Dream* (Stratford, Ontario), *The Philanthropist* (Broadway), *The American Plan* (Broadway), *Crown Matrimonial* (Tour), *Blackbird* (Tour), *Pygmalion* (Broadway), *Journey's End* (Broadway) which won the 2007 Tony Award for Best Revival. *In The Club* (Hampstead/ Tour), *Honour* (Wyndham's), *The Philanthropist* (Donmar), *National Anthems* (Old Vic), *What The Butler Saw* (Hampstead/Criterion), *Some*

*Girls* (Gielgud), *Journey's End* (Comedy), *Abigail's Party* (Hampstead/Whitehall), *Loot* (Chichester/Vaudeville), *Single Spies* (Tour), *Richard III* (Colchester) and *The League of Gentlemen*.

### Jonathan Fensom | Designer

Theatre credits include: *The Goat/Any Given Day* (Traverse), *Philadelphia Here I Come* (Dublin), *Brighton Beach Memoirs* (Watford Palace); *Six Degrees Of Separation* (Old Vic); *Rain Man, Some Girls, Twelfth Night, Smaller, Blackbird* (West End), *Henry IV, King Lear, Love's Labour's Lost* (Globe), *Swan Lake* (San Francisco Ballet), *Journey's End* (West End, Broadway), *The American Plan, Pygmalion* (New York), *The Homecoming, Big White Fog* (Almeida), *A Midsummer Night's Dream* (Canada), *Crown Matrimonial* (Guildford, Tour), *Faith Healer* (Dublin).

### Jason Taylor | Lighting Designer

Theatre credits include: *The Empire* (Royal Court), *Six Degrees of Separation* (Old Vic), *The Merry Wives of Windsor* (Globe Theatre USA/UK tour), *The Rivals* (Theatre Royal Bath/Tour/West End), *Rainman* (West End/tour), *The Good Soldier* (Ustinov, Bath), *Noises Off* (Birmingham Rep), *The Big Fellah* (Out of Joint), *Charley's Aunt* (Manchester Royal Exchange), *Brighton Beach Memoirs* (Watford Palace), *Rum and Coca Cola* (West Yorkshire Playhouse/ETT tour), *Absurd Person Singular* (West End/UK tour), *Duet For One* (West End/tour), and *Flashdance* (UK tour).

### Gregory Clarke | Sound Designer

Gregory won a Tony Award for Best Sound Design in a Play for *Equus* and received the New York Drama Desk Award for Outstanding Sound Design for *Journey's End*. Theatre credits include: *Twelfth Night, Earthquakes in London* (National), *A Flea In Her Ear, Six Degrees of Separation* (Old Vic), *Penelope* (Druid Theatre), *Bedroom Farce* (West End), *Rain Man* (West End), *Peter Pan* (Kensington/O2/US), *Goodnight Mister Tom, A Month In The Country* (Chichester), *A Midsummer Night's Dream, Treasure Island, Bedroom Farce/Miss Julie, Love's Labour's Lost* (Rose); *The Philanthropist* (Broadway), *For King And Country* (UK Tour), *The Electric Ballroom* (Riverside), *Crown Matrimonial, Ring Around the Moon* (Act Productions), *Equus* (Gielgud & Broadway), *The Rivals, Balmoral, Swansong, How the Other Half Loves, HMS Pinafore, Much Ado About Nothing, As You Like It* (Bath), *Where There's A Will, Uncle Vanya* (ETT); *Peter Pan, Krindlekrax* (Birmingham), *Lady Be Good, A Midsummer Night's Dream, Macbeth, Twelfth Night, Cymbeline* (NSC).

**Miranda Foster** | Dramaturg

Miranda worked with Jonathan Lewis over 18 months on a re-write of the play. As an actress her most recent credit is playing Gertrude in the Shakespeare's Globe production of Hamlet directed by Dominic Dromgoole and Bill Buckhurst, which toured in the UK prior to a New York season.

**Stephen Moore** CDG | Casting Director

Theatre includes: *Some White Chick* (Southwark Playhouse), *Ordinary Dreams* (Trafalgar Studios), *Midnight Cowboy* (Assembly Rooms, Edinburgh), *Miss Dis'Grace & Diamond Johnny Ray* (Edinburgh), *The Exonerated* (Riverside Studios), *Perpetua* (Theatre 503). Television includes: *Father Brown* (BBC), *Land Girls* (BBC), *Dawson Bros Funtime* (BBC), *EastEnders* (BBC), *Doctors* (BBC). Further TV credits as Assistant Casting Director include: *Rome* (HBO/BBC), *Longford* (HBO/Channel 4), *The Virgin Queen* (BBC), *He Knew He Was Right* (BBC), *Byron* (BBC), *Final Demand* (BBC), *Eroica* (BBC), *Suspicion* (ITV1), *Jeffrey Archer: The Truth* (BBC), *The Inspector Lynley Mysteries* (BBC), *Bertie & Elizabeth* (ITV1). Film includes: *The Contractor*. As Casting Associate: *Starter for Ten*, *Amazing Grace*, *Brothers of the Head*. As Casting Assistant: *Hot Fuzz*, *The Good Night*, *Big Nothing*, *Flightplan*, *The Illusionist*, *Imagine Me & You*, *Sahara*, *The Heart of Me*, *I Capture the Castle*, *Bend It Like Beckham*. Short Film includes: *Chicken Soup*, *Earthquake*, *Ela*. Stephen is a member of the Casting Directors' Guild of Great Britain.

**Katherine Hare** | Assistant Director

Directing credits include the UK Premiere of *Bernarda Alba* at The Union Theatre for Triptic, *Bad Musical* for The Trap (Edinburgh Fringe), *The Tender Land* at the Arcola Theatre, *Crazy for You* at The London Palladium, *The Beach* at the Cockpit Theatre and *Modern Dance for Beginners* at the Camden People's Theatre. Assisting and associate credits include *Park Avenue Cat* at the Arts Theatre, *Dirty White Boy* at Trafalgar Studios, *Proud* at the New Wimbledon Studio and the UK tour of *Hit Me: The Life and Rhymes of Ian Dury* that also enjoyed a run at the Garrick Theatre, West End. Katherine is a founder member and artistic director of Triptic www.triptictheatre.com.

**Paul Bouchier** | Company Stage Manager

Since graduating from the GSA Stage Management course in 1991 Paul is enjoying a varied career in theatre, television, film and events. Theatre credits include the recent UK tour of *I Dreamed A Dream, The Susan Boyle Musical*, *Chess* (UK Tour, Italy and Princess of Wales Theatre, Toronto), *Rent* (Shaftesbury Theatre), *The Phantom of the Opera*, *Buddy, The Buddy Holly Story* (Victoria Palace Theatre, Strand Theatre and UK Tour), *The Magistrate* (Chichester Festival Theatre), *An Ideal Husband* and *Women Laughing* (Royal Exchange Theatre, Manchester). As a First or Second Assistant Director or Floor Manager television and film credits include *Coronation Street* (5 years), *Stars in their Eyes*, *A&E*, *The Catherine Tate Show*, *Summer*, *RIBA Stirling Prize*, *An Angel for May* and *Building The Titanic* plus numerous pilots and commercials. Paul has also worked for Manchester International Festival since its first year in 2007 and various events all over the UK.

**Briony Allen** | Deputy Stage Manager

Briony trained at Guildhall School of Music and Drama. Theatre credits include: *Ragtime* (Regent's Park Open Air Theatre), *The Ladykillers* (Liverpool Playhouse/Gielgud), *Love Never Dies* (Adelphi), *Passion* (Donmar Warehouse), *The Fantasticks* (Duchess), *Cat on a Hot Tin Roof* (Novello), *Peter Pan* (Kensington Gardens), *Zorro the Musical* (UK Tour/Garrick), *Imagine This* (Theatre Royal, Plymouth), *Footloose the Musical* (UK Tour/Novello), *Annie Get Your Gun* (UK Tour), *Fame the Musical* (UK Tour), *Saturday Night Fever* (UK Tour/Apollo Victoria), *Romeo and Juliet the Musical* (Piccadilly), *Noises Off* (Comedy), *Peggy Sue Got Married* (Shaftesbury), *Buried Alive*, *Keepers*, *On the Whole*, *Ancient Lights*, *Good Samaritan*, *Speaking in Tongues*, *Burning Issues*, *Flesh and Blood*, *Gone to LA*, *Peggy For You* (Hampstead Theatre).

**Gareth Johnson** | Production Consultant

In stage, company, production and general management as well as production consultancy and as a producer Gareth Johnson has worked on over 100 productions in the West End and on tour with producers including Michael Codron, Nica Burns, Thelma Holt, Lee Menzies, Tara Arts, Mark Rubinstein, Lee Dean, Act Productions and Stoll Moss Theatres. Directors and writers worked with include Sir Alan Ayckbourn, Michael Frayn, Simon Gray, Harold Pinter, Sir Tom Stoppard, Sir Ronald Harwood, Peter Dews, Peter Wood, Sir Trevor Nunn, David Grindley, Timothy Sheader, Gale Edwards, Jatinder Verma, Simon Callow, Athol Fugard, Michael

Blakemore, Alan Strachan, Richard Wilson, Sam Mendes, Michael Rudman, Patrick Marber, and Anthony Minghella. He has also worked as an actor at reps such as Birmingham, on TV and radio in plays, serials and series such as *Troubleshooters*, *Trial*, *Cause Célèbre* and *The Archers*. He serves on the boards of Tara Arts and Theatr Mwldan, and has worked with Arts Council of Wales in an advisory capacity. He devised and runs annually a course at RADA about producing and general management.

## James Seabright for Seabright Productions | Producer

Seabright Productions is a theatre production and general management company based in London's West End. As well as being one of the busiest presenters of UK tours on the small and middle scale circuits, recent London production and management projects include *Potted Potter* (Trafalgar Studios 2007-9, Garrick 2011, world tour 2012), *Potted Panto* (Vaudeville 2010/11), *Showstopper! The Improvised Musical* (Ambassadors 2011, Criterion 2011, Southbank 2010/11/12 and Kings Head 2009/10), *Hit Me* (Garrick 2010), *Barbershopera* (Trafalgar Studios 2010/11), *The Fitzrovia Radio Hour* (Trafalgar Studios 2011, Ambassadors 2012), *Terror* (Southwark Playhouse 2009/10, Soho 2011), and *Dirty White Boy* (Trafalgar Studios 2010). Producer James Seabright's book *So You Want To Be A Theatre Producer* was published in the UK in 2010 and in North America in 2011. James has produced and promoted over 150 productions at the Edinburgh Fringe since 2001, winning various awards including The Herald Angel and The Scotsman Fringe First. He co-founded the Festival Highlights producers' alliance in 2003, which has since grown to be the largest independent promoter of shows at the largest arts festival in the world. James has twice been the recipient of the Stage One New Producer Bursary (2002 and 2004), is a member of the Society of London Theatre, and has been a guest speaker at RADA, City Lit and at the Masterclass series run by Theatre Royal Haymarket.

| | |
|---|---|
| Assistant Producer | **Claire Turner** (Stage One Apprentice) |
| Associate Producers | **Kat Portman** |
| | **Simon Cummin** |
| Business Manager | **Andy Farrell** |
| Press Representative | **Kate Gambrell** |
| Producer | **James Seabright** |

| | |
|---|---|
| Office | Palace Theatre, Shaftesbury Avenue, London W1D 5AY |
| Telephone | +44 20 7439 1173 |
| Fax | +44 20 7183 6023 |
| Email | office@seabrights.com |
| Web | www.seabrights.com |

**Jenny Topper** | Producer

Jenny Topper was Artistic Director of Hampstead Theatre until 2003. During her time there she produced some 126 plays, 41 of which had a further life in the West End, on Broadway, or on tour.

Notable transfers to the West End: *A Room Of One's Own* with Eileen Atkins; *What The Butler Saw*, *Burn This* by Lanford Wilson, with John Malkovich and Juliet Stevenson, *Someone Who'll Watch Over Me* by Frank McGuinness, *Dead Funny* by Terry Johnson, with Niall Buggy, David Haig and Zoë Wanamaker, *The Memory of Water* by Shelagh Stephenson, *Little Malcolm and His Struggle Against the Eunuchs* by David Halliwell, with Ewan McGregor and Mike Leigh's *Abigail's Party* — a silver jubilee production of Hampstead Theatre's most famous play and the final play in the theatre's old building.

Prior to Hampstead Theatre, Jenny was for more than 10 years an Artistic Director of the Bush Theatre. During her time there Jenny produced the work of numerous writers such as John Byrne, Kevin Elyot, Lucy Gannon, Robert Holman, Dusty Hughes, Terry Johnson, Tom Kempinski, Sharman Macdonald and Billy Roche.

Having commissioned and opened the new Hampstead Theatre, Jenny went on to produce *Sweet Panic* by Stephen Poliakoff, two tours of *Abigail's Party*, *The Goat* by Edward Albee, with Jonathan Pryce and Eddie Redmayne, the acclaimed production of Albee's *Who's Afraid of Virginia Woolf?*, starring Kathleen Turner, *Martha, Josie and the Chinese Elvis* by Charlotte Jones, with Maureen Lipman, *Terms of Endearment*, with Linda Gray and Suranne Jones, *The Clean House* by Sarah Ruhl, with Eleanor Bron and Patricia Hodge, *Duet for One* by Tom Kempinski (Almeida and Vaudeville) with Henry Goodman and Juliet Stevenson and *End Of The Rainbow* by Peter Quilter and starring Tracie Bennett (West End, Tour and On Broadway).

**Sue Scott Davison** | Producer

Following over 25 years as an actress, Sue was awarded a Stage One New Producer's Bursary in 2004. She won a Meridian Theatre Interact Award for the development and production of Glyn Maxwell's *Liberty*, which she co-produced with Shakespeare's Globe in 2008, followed by a national tour. Other productions include: *After Troy* (Oxford Playhouse and Shaw Theatre 2011), *Future Me* (Theatre 503 and National Tour 2007/9), *Two Way Mirror* (Courtyard Theatre, 2006), and *The Lifeblood* (Edinburgh Festival and Riverside Studios 2004/5). Sue has recently co-produced the critically acclaimed and Lawrence Olivier award winning *The Railway Children* at Waterloo Station (2010-12) as well as the production in Toronto (2011).

**Lee Menzies | Producer**

Current productions include: the first ever stage version of Irving Berlin's musical *Top Hat* (Aldwych Theatre, London), the third West End production of *Yes, Prime Minister* (Trafalgar Studios) and a national tour of Noel Gay's musical *Radio Times*. In development are the musical of *From Here to Eternity* which he is co-producing with Tim Rice who has written the lyrics for the production, and a new play by BBC journalist Gavin Esler.

Most recent productions include: Leonard Bernstein's *Wonderful Town* (national tour), the third national tour of *Yes, Prime Minister*, *Crazy For You* (Novello Theatre, Olivier Award Winner for Best Revival), David Grindley's multi award-winning production of *Journey's End* at the Duke of York's Theatre and on tour, Dominic West in Simon Gray's *Butley* (Duchess Theatre), Andrew Lloyd Webber and Don Black's definitive version of *Tell Me on a Sunday* on tour and a new production of the Noël Coward revue *Cowardy Custard*, *Yes, Prime Minister* (Apollo and Gielgud Theatre), the multi award-winning *Jerusalem* starring Mark Rylance (Apollo), *Enron* (Broadhurst, New York), *Prick Up Your Ears* (Comedy), *Twelfth Night* (Noël Coward), Otherwise Engaged (UK tour and Criterion), *Donkeys' Years* (Comedy, three Olivier Award nominations including Best Revival), *Whipping It Up* with Richard Wilson (Ambassadors, Olivier Award nomination for Best New Comedy), *Pete and Dud: Come Again* (The Venue) and *Footloose* (Playhouse). Also, four productions with Peter Hall — *Twelfth Night*, *The Rose Tattoo* with Julie Walters and Ken Stott, *Tartuffe* with Paul Eddington, Felicity Kendall, John Sessions, Toby Stephens and Jennifer Ehle, and *Hedda Gabler* with Fiona Shaw (Olivier Award for Best Revival), the Young Vic production of *An Enemy of the People* (Playhouse), Donald Sinden as Oscar Wilde in *Diversions and Delights* and Eileen Atkins as Virginia Woolf in *A Room of One's Own* (Playhouse), *Over My Shoulder* (Wyndham's), Neil LaBute's *The Shape of Things* (New Ambassadors), Jeffrey Archer's three plays *Beyond Reasonable Doubt* (Queen's), *Exclusive* (Novello) and *The Accused* (Theatre Royal, Haymarket), *Our Town* with Alan Alda (Shaftesbury), *Dry Rot* (Lyric), *I Love You, You're Perfect, Now Change* (Comedy), the NT production of *The Island* (Old Vic and UK tour, EMMA Award), *Jus' Like That!* (Garrick and three UK tours), *High Society* (Shaftesbury) and *Kat and the Kings* (Vaudeville, New York Cort, Frankfurt and UK tour, eight Olivier Awards including Best New Musical).

UK tours include: *Beyond Reasonable Doubt*, *Daisy Pulls It Off*, *Gasping*, *The Shell Seekers*, *The Accused*, *Anything Goes*, *The Wedding Singer* and *Crown Matrimonial*.

He is the second longest serving member of The Society's Finance and Business Affairs Standing Committee, a member of The Society's Investment Committee, a trustee of The Society's Staff Pension Fund and chairman of The Laurence Olivier Bursary panel. From 1988 to 1992 he was Managing Director of the Playhouse, Northumberland Avenue under the chairmanship of Lord Havers and subsequently Lord Rix. He remained as a consultant to the theatre until it was sold in 1996 by Ray Cooney. He was a governor at the Central School of Speech and Drama for the maximum nine year term and is a member of the board of Tara Arts, the leading Anglo-Indian theatre company.

www.leemenzies.co.uk

For Lee Menzies Ltd:

| | |
|---|---|
| General Manager | **Gareth Johnson** |
| Associate Producer | **Jacob Wagen** |
| Production Coordinator | **Carla Morris** |

The text of the play was correct at the time of going to press while rehearsals were still in progress.

# ACT I

## Scene 1

*Ward 9 Bay 4 of the Queen Elizabeth Military Hospital, Woolwich. Early Spring, 1984. Late afternoon*

*The wards are divided into bays and single rooms, the single rooms being for officers. Each ward has eight bays and usually a half male, half female ratio. Each bay has four beds*

*There is one entrance to the bay, in the centre of the back wall. To either side of the entrance are glass panels through which the corridor beyond can be seen. The corridor ends to the L, so the bay can only be approached from the R. To the L of the door is a bath chair, to the R a pedal bin*

*Four beds are visible; each is placed diagonally in a corner of the room with its foot pointing C. All but the UL bed has a cabinet beside it. Above each bed the name of the occupant is written in black marker pen. The name PO Menzies is written above the bed UL; this bed is unoccupied. UR is Keith's bed; those DL and DR are occupied by Joe and Ian respectively. The occupied beds are surrounded by belongings; Joe's cabinet-top is notable for the meticulous arrangement of his personal items, a mirror, comb, bottle of aftershave, hairbrush, can of spray deodorant, framed photograph and photograph album. Keith's cabinet has on it a Walkman and an electronic pocket chess game, amongst other items. Ian's cabinet has on it a fruit bowl and a "curly wurly" drinking straw — as used by patients with feeding difficulties — and several get well cards are Blutacked to its sides. There is a plastic chair beside Ian's cabinet*

*The other major item of furniture in the room is a television set which stands on a low trolley at the foot of Ian's bed, facing the rest of the room*

*Other hospital apparatus — bedpans, patients' charts, jugs of water, glasses, etc. — are distributed around the room in appropriate places*

*Under a sound-bite montage of events and chart music from the early 80s, which should sound something like a radio turning through different stations, we hear a snare drum doing a military pattern. (It would be nice if the montage could include Thatcher's famous response to the capture of*

*part of the Falkland Islands, "Rejoice at that news" and Reagan's, "You
ain't seen nothing yet" followed by his supporters chanting, "Four more
years".) The montage fades and the drumming gets louder and louder*

*Joe enters furtively, carrying an army suitcase. He puts it on to his bed and
opens it. He gets out several cans of lager and a gift-wrapped box containing
a blow-up doll. He puts the beers in his bedside cabinet and the box under
the bed. He is just finishing this as Keith enters, making him jump*

*The drumming stops*

**Keith**  A Rupert! I can't believe they'd do that to us. A fucking Rupert,
Jesus!

**Joe**  Sheila asked if it was all right.

**Keith**  And you said yes? I might have known it was you. Well thank
you for remembering I live here too. A fucking Rupert!

**Joe**  She needed to know straightaway. And you weren't here.

**Keith**  Well?

**Joe**  Well what?

**Keith**  Did you get it?

**Joe**  Yeah.

**Keith**  Which one?

**Joe**  Mandy.

**Keith**  Mandy! Which one was Mandy?

**Joe**  You'll have to wait and see. (*He throws the case to Keith*)

*Keith puts the case behind his bed*

I got it gift wrapped. And I borrowed a few beers. He's getting a bit
greedy he is. Parry's mate in the Naafi. Ten quid he wanted for this
gear, but I only had seven left, so I told him to like it or lump it.

**Keith**  Cheeky fucker.

**Joe**  He wants another five to get rid of the empties now. He's getting
like Al Ca-fucking-pone. Just because he's a full screw he thinks he
rules the roost.

**Keith**  I thought he was a Lance-Jack.

**Joe**  No. He's got two stripes all right, has Corporal Wince. He probably
bought them though.

**Keith**  (*pointing at Joe's cabinet*) Ah, we can't do that no more, not with
a Rupert in the bay. No way.

**Joe**  Course we can. Anyway, he's not a real Rupert, he's a PO.

**Keith**  A potential Rupert! That's even worse. There's plenty of single
rooms — why does she have to put him in here? They never put an
officer in with us before.

**Joe** I said we'd do Sheila a favour.

**Keith** A favour? You make it sound like a weeny little thing. This is a fucking big IOU.

**Joe** (*smiling*) Exactly. We scratch her back, and she can massage warm baby oil into ours.

*Joe starts to get changed out of his tracksuit and into a smart casual shirt and trousers*

**Keith** I still don't like it. (*Pause*) He'll be wanting the music turned down. What about the video? We'll probably have to spend the whole time watching wildlife documentaries.

**Joe** Look, she's had trouble with him all week. He hasn't been sticking to his bed rest.

**Keith** Excuse me, and where are we off to now?

**Joe** Oh are you coming and all?

**Keith** You've only been back five minutes. This isn't the fucking Hilton you know.

**Joe** Terrible, isn't it, hospital? It can really get you down.

**Keith** Well I hope your evening's as much fun as mine.

**Joe** I'm only going down the *Tuns*. I'll be back for the match. I tell you what though, you wouldn't video the "Street" for us would you?

**Keith** Fuck off!

**Joe** Go on.

**Keith** Fuck off ——

*Potential Officer Oliver Menzies (pronounced Mingies) — known as POM — enters. He has a noticeable bulge at the base of his spine under his pyjamas. He is wheeling his bedside cabinet. He pushes it between his bed and the bath chair, then hobbles off, walking with great difficulty*

What did I tell you? He's gone to get his fucking sofa!

*POM enters with a number of plastic bags containing the rest of his things, including a bottle of Ribena and a towel, his wash kit, a copy of* Time Out *and some other magazines, an address book, an apple and a jumper*

*Keith puts his earphones on, switches on some very loud heavy metal music and starts to play with his electronic pocket chess set. Keith and Joe watch POM unpack. His towel falls on to the floor*

*Just as POM reaches the towel Joe comes over and picks it up*

Thank you. (*He takes the towel from Joe and dusts it off during the following*)

**Joe** Don't worry we're not the NHS here! I'm Joe.

**POM** Second Lieutenant Menzies.

**Joe** I thought it was potential Second Lieutenant.

**POM** Well, yes. Technically. (*Pause*) Been here long?

**Joe** Twenty-two months. (*He sprays deodorant under his arms*)

**POM** Twenty-two months! You've been here twenty-two months?

**Joe** Twenty-one months and three weeks, but I like to round it up. Hyde Park, July eighty-two. Trooper Joe Morgan 1st Battalion Blues and Royals. (*He sprays deodorant on his pubic hair*)

**POM** Household Cavalry. Are your lot on ceremonials then?

**Joe** Yeah, Chelsea. They've just come down from Windsor. I haven't been with them for a while though.

**Keith** Ha! Check!

**Joe** (*meaning Keith*) And this is Wank. No, really it is. It's an old Irish name. He's Irish you see. Irish Rangers. His mum named him after Hank Wangford. She was into Country and Western.

*A beat. Keith starts to sing along to his tape*

He's partially deaf actually. Perforated hearing they call it, and he loves his music — that's why it's so loud. At least some of it gets through! Back in a minute sir. Managed to wangle an evening pass, just got to get it signed by Hatchet-Face.

**POM** Hatchet-Face?

**Joe** Sister.

**POM** Oh Hatchet-Face. (*He smiles*) Very good. You're allowed to go out?

**Joe** Yeah, but you've got to be careful. (*He holds up a packet of condoms. Then, to Keith*) All right, Wank?

*Joe exits*

**Keith** (*looking up*) What?

*Keith sees Joe leave but doesn't know what he said because of the earphones. Suddenly Keith is violently drumming the air; then there is silence. He turns his Walkman off, takes the headphones off, turns on his side and continues to play with his pocket chess set, his back to the POM*

*POM discovers he has no water in his bedside jug to add to his Ribena. He presses his help button by the side of his bed but nothing happens.*

*He tries the button again, but still nothing. He starts to hobble, but feels a twinge, and looks towards Keith*

**POM** Excuse me, Wank?

*No response*

I'm sorry to disturb you.

*Still no response*

Would you mind pressing your help button for me — Wank?

*Keith turns slowly to look at him, then turns back*

**Keith** (*turning to POM again*) Are you talking to me?
**POM** Oh I'm sorry you probably can't hear me can you? Can you hear me?
**Keith** Ay, I heard you.
**POM** Good. Um. (*He points to Keith's help button*) Help button Wank. Er. Press.

*Pause. There is no reply. Keith just stares at him*

(*Pressing the palm of his hand with his index finger*) Water! Can you lip read?
**Keith** Right that's it, I'm sorry but that's it. (*He gets off his bed*) Potential Officer or not, I'm not having that. We'll see about this ...

*Keith exits*

*POM is left wondering what the problem is. He goes stealthily over to Keith's bed and helps himself to some water from Keith's jug for his Ribena. He then hobbles quickly away from the bed, stands in the middle of the bay and takes a large sip. He notices the TV on the trolley by the fourth bed in the bay and turns it on. The programme is a wildlife documentary which we hear for a few seconds; then POM turns over to snooker on BBC2. He much prefers this and mounts his own bed to watch it*

*Ian enters. He is in a wheelchair and appears to be little more than a vegetable. (But as the play progresses so does his recovery, including the way he speaks, which is very slow and deliberate to begin with.) He has a noticeable, recent scar on his temple. He sits right in front of the screen leaving POM watching the back of Ian's head*

**Keith**  I wouldn't make yourself too at home here. I've told Sheila all
about this. Potential Officer or not I take great exception to being
called a wanker and shouted at. That's a very black mark against you
sir. Sheila's consulting with Hatchet-Face. I expect they'll try and
move you before tea. (*To Ian*) Calling me a wanker.

**POM**  It's not Wank is it?

**Keith**  You tell me!

**POM**  Hank Wankford?

**Keith**  What kind of medication are you on?

**POM**  He told me you were called ——

*Ian moans loudly which surprises POM. Keith is used to these noises*

*Joe enters*

**Keith**  I'd lie still if I were you. I'm sure they won't be long.

**Joe**  (*to POM*) Has he been bothering you? (*He raises his voice and does
made-up sign language to Keith*) Wank? Have you been bothering
him? I'm sorry sir. He gets these funny turns. Forgets his own name
sometimes, doesn't he Ian? Pretends he's not even deaf. Like when
Donald Pleasence pretends he can see in The Great Escape. You know,
the scene with James Garner and the needle on the floor. You must
know that sir. That's a classic. The Great Escape. Steve McQueen. The
motorbike scene?

**Keith**  Ha bloody ha. (*To POM*) And do you know what we call him?
"The Battersea Boner".

**POM**  "Battersea Boner"?

**Keith**  Work it out. There's a dog's home in Battersea. (*To Joe*) No
wonder they had to take your finger off. God knows what diseases
you've picked up.

**Joe**  Oh, I nearly forgot, I've got a message from Hatchet-Face. As our
new member of Bay 4 is only going to be with us for a few weeks
would we help to make his stay a pleasant one. And that wasn't a
request — Keith. (*Beat*) Would anyone like anything while I'm out?
No. Well, have a nice evening gents.

**Ian**  Twenty Benson.

**Joe**  How many?

**Ian**  Twenty Benson. (*He slowly reaches inside a pocket for a fiver*)

**Joe**  How many?

**Ian**  You heard.

**Joe**  Well you've got to practise haven't you?

**Ian**  (*struggling to get the words out*) Fuck off!

**Joe**  You are getting better.

*Ian can't get the money out*

It's all right, I'll get these. Just get him to video the "Street", 'cause I'm very worried about Mavis. (*He heads for the exit; to Keith, waving*) Bye Wank.

*Joe exits*

**Keith** Fuck off! (*Pause*) It's Keith, actually. My name's Keith. So we better get that straight for starters.
**POM** Right. Keith.
**Keith** What did they want to put you in here for anyway? I thought youse officers always got the single rooms.
**POM** Oh. Um ... I offered. There's a Major's wife with ingrowing toenails.
**Keith** It wouldn't have anything to do with not staying on bed rest then?
**POM** Sorry?
**Keith** Nothing.
**POM** (*after a pause*) So, you're Irish then?
**Keith** No I'm not.
**POM** But you've got an Irish accent.
**Keith** Well spotted!
**POM** Is Hank Wankford Irish?
**Keith** I just said I'm not Irish. I'm British. Ever heard of the Orangemen?
**POM** William of Orange and the battle of the Boyne, yes.
**Keith** Ay, but do you know about the Orangemen?
**POM** Oh yes. The six counties and all that. I mean it's the other way round, isn't it? If you're not um ...
**Keith** (*letting POM trail off; disgusted*) Excuse me. I've got to make a phone-call.

*Keith exits*

(*From the corridor*) Inland!

*Gunner Michael "Mick" Speedy and Fusilier Parry wheel themselves into the bay like a whirlwind*

**Mick** All right "E"?
**Parry** All right Ian?

*Ian looks up*

Excuse me sir. Have you seen him? Wank?

*Parry, Mick and Ian laugh*

**POM** He's gone to make a phone call.

**Parry** You must be the bum case Sheila was talking about.

**POM** It's the base of my spine.

**Parry** Same difference. Did they pack it?

**POM** Sorry?

**Parry** Pilunidal sinuses. They usually pack them. Unless it's really deep. Then you're in big trouble.

**Mick** They have to dress them a couple of times a day. Very painful it is.

**Parry** Very ugly. I've seen them put (*he holds his arms outstretched*) that much cotton wool up there.

**Mick** Easy. I've seen them put about twenty-five foot of it in that REME Lance-Jack before now.

**Parry** What do you expect from a REME Lance-Jack, all day on his backside under an engine. And it recurred.

**POM** Really?

**Parry** Oh yes. Apparently there's always a fifty-fifty chance it will recur.

**POM** Well, you do seem to be very up on pilunidal sinuses.

**Parry** That's because my last Company Commander died of one.

**POM** What?

**Parry** Got you there! No, you're all right. You see, they only have problems if they don't catch it early enough. Because the ingrowing hair that causes it, when it's ingrowing up your bum it grows so long that it starts rubbing against your anus. (*He picks up POM's chart from the end of his bed and studies it*)

**Mick** (*pulling a terrible face*) All that pus and shit.

**Parry** Yeah look, they packed it. Deep tension stitches through the muscles. Keep your bum cheeks from closing. Less chance of infection.

**POM** (*taking the chart back from Parry*) Yes, I do know.

**Parry** Fusilier Parry.

**POM** Sorry?

**Parry** That's me. Fusilier Parry.

**Mick** But everyone calls him Fuckhead! (*He laughs*)

*The others just look at him*

You know. Wank! Fuckhead!

**Parry** All right. We had the joke. Had the laugh, and now we've moved on. (*To Ian*) Fuckhead!

**Mick** And I'm Gunner Speedy sir. We're in Bay 2. Well, we're not in Bay 2 at the moment, because we're talking to you obviously ——

**Parry**  See what I have to put up with? Unbelievable! You're the PO then?
**POM**  Yes, my name's Oliver.
**Mick**  Oh I'm sorry.

*There is an embarrassed silence*

**POM**  REME. That's Royal Electrical and Mechanical Engineers isn't it?
**Parry**  No, Rough Engineering Made Easy.
**Mick**  And remember — "If Jim can't fix it ...
**Mick**  ⎫
**Parry**  ⎬ (*together*) REME can!"
**POM**  Very funny. All these abbreviations. Can't get used to them. PO, MO, QEMH. It's like learning another language isn't it?
**Mick**  You have to have abbreviations. (*He recites the following as if he has learnt it*) It reduces personal inefficiencies in a large and diverse organization, but it shouldn't be thought of as dehumanizing.
**Parry**  Well, well, well, Mr Fucking Psychology. You been saving that one up?
**Mick**  No, we done a course on it just before I left Junior Leaders. "The Army, a Total Institution". It was brilliant. We done all this brain-washing techniques and hypnotics.
**Parry**  You what?
**Mick**  A.E.I.O.U. Accuracy, Efficiency, Immediacy, Organization ... U. Can't remember the U.
**POM**  Unforgettable?
**Mick**  No it wasn't unforgettable. Undetected, Undetectable? (*Beat*) Because you see in the field communication is of the utmost importance.
**POM**  What field?
**Mick**  *The* field. For example, if your Battalion HQ, Adjutant, or RSM wanted to send you a get well card they wouldn't send it to Potential Officer Menzies, Ward 9 Bay 4, Queen Elizabeth Military Hospital, would they?
**POM**  Wouldn't they?
**Mick**  No. They'd send it to PO Menzies W9B4 QEMH. Yeah, abbreviations are a good technique.
**POM**  You pronounce it Mingies not Menzies.
**Mick**  Why do you spell it like that then?
**POM**  It's always been spelt like that.
**Mick**  Yeah, but you don't say John Mingies do you? "I've just popped down to John Mingies." You say John Menzies.
**POM**  Why do you spell Lieutenant Lieutenant but pronounce it "Leftenant"?

**Mick**  Yeah, but the Americans don't do that though do they?

**Parry**  What are you talking about? Did you have all your brains in your foreskin? He had to come in for the chop. Moby Dick here had to have half of it chopped off. Too big.

**Mick**  Fuck off! I'm sorry sir.

**POM**  No, don't mind me.

**Mick**  The MO decided I needed to be circumcised for health and hygiene.

**Parry**  Yeah, he kept choking all the sheep!

**Mick**  I kept getting infections under the foreskin.

**Parry**  So they whipped it off and now he's got no brains! Baaah! Here, how about giving Mr — how does it go again?

**POM**  Mingies.

**Parry**  How about giving Mr Mingies a quick peek?

**Mick**  What?

**Parry**  Give him a little flash. Show him your trimmings.

**Mick**  I'm sure Mr Menzies doesn't share your perversions, Parry.

**Parry**  Go on — you want to see it don't you sir?

**POM**  If Gunner Speedy doesn't.

**Parry**  You see. Course he does.

**Mick**  (*to POM*) Why do you want to have a look? What are you going to do?

**Parry**  Nothing. We just want to have a look. It's very interesting actually, sir, from a medical point of view, to see a newly circumcised one in the wild, so to speak.

**Mick**  All right, but you can't touch. It's still very sensitive.

*Mick wheels himself closer to POM's bed, Parry moves in, and even Ian wheels himself over to have a look. They are in a huddle. Mick unties his waist cord*

**Parry**  Jesus Christ, look at the Hampton on him.

**Mick**  Get off Ian. What are you trying to do?

**Parry**  He's a big boy, our Gunner Speedy.

**Mick**  Knock it on the head, Parry.

**Parry**  Well we can't knock it on the foreskin can we!

**POM**  Looks like you've been bitten. Is it supposed to be that black?

**Mick**  That's the bruising and the stitches. I've heard it makes it more sensitive. Gives the ladies a smoother finish. I'll let you know.

**Parry**  They'll just think you're a fucking yid.

**Mick**  No, I haven't got the nose for it, and I don't support Tottenham Hotspur. (*He laughs at his own joke*)

**Parry**  That's God's punishment for crucifying Jesus.

**POM**  What, supporting Tottenham Hotspur?

**Parry** (*ignoring POM's attempt at a joke*) Don't they get the chop when they're babies? Just think about it, one slip by the Rabbi and a he could end up a she for the rest of his life. Very painful.

**POM** They don't feel a thing actually, they're only a few days old. And it's done by doctors.

**Mick** You know a lot about it sir.

**Parry** The advantages of an education, Michael.

**POM** The advantages of being Jewish.

*There is a pause while Mick wheels himself closer to POM and scrutinizes his face*

**Mick** You don't look it.

*Ian laughs*

**POM** So how long's it been since the operation?

**Mick** Week tomorrow.

**Parry** And it's still painful? (*He winks at POM*)

**Mick** Is it painful! Mornings are terrible. Fucking terrible.

**Parry** That's a bit unusual isn't it sir, a week?

**POM** And they haven't said anything?

**Mick** Said what? What?

**Parry** One way or the other?

**Mick** What do you mean one way or the other?

**Parry** Whether it's been successful.

**Mick** What do you mean successful?

**Parry** Well, you know in some cases it can grow back.

**Mick** Grow back! Don't make me laugh.

**Parry** Can't it sir?

**POM** I've heard it said in some quarters

**Parry** Ian?

**Ian** Yeah.

**Parry** Thank you.

**Mick** You mean I could have gone through all this agony for nothing? You're winding me up.

**Parry** No, no, no, not on something as serious as this, Mick. Honestly, there was this Colour Sergeant in our Battalion — he had it done last year. Came back to work, they thought it was all right, but he started getting really edgy when we had to get changed for sport. It got to the point where he'd break out in a cold sweat. Then I noticed his trousers starting to bulge. I thought he must have had a permanent hard-on. Then one morning, he didn't turn up for work. They'd rushed him back in. He couldn't hide it any longer. Do you know what it was?

**Mick**  What?

**POM**  What?

**Parry**  It's very very very rare. Foreskinnus Nonstoppus.

**Mick**  What's that?

**Parry**  Well, it's a bit like Coitus Interruptus or when you have your hair
cut. It stimulates the hair to grow back, but it grows back thicker and
faster. Well the same thing can happen to your foreskin as well, especially
if you've had the chop later on in life. You know — like ——

**Parry** }
**POM** } (*together*) Early twenties.

**Mick**  I'm early twenties!

**Parry**  Yeah, he was a nice bloke, our Nobby.

**Mick**  What happened to him?

**Parry**  Dunno. Never saw him again.

**Mick**  You're having me on. You're joking aren't you? That can't happen
— can it?

**Parry**  It may still be too early to tell.

**Mick**  They would have told me. I'd sue them, I'd sue the fucking Army.
They made me do it. I wouldn't have done it otherwise.

**Parry**  You can't sue the Army Michael.

**POM**  No. You wouldn't have a leg to stand on.

**Mick**  Do you think that's why that nurse always comes to check when I
have to have a piss? I couldn't even hold it the first time I went. He had
to bring a bucket, and it was going everywhere, all over him.

**Parry**  What? That big yellow bucket in the corridor? Urgh!

**Mick**  Yeah and this nurse was squatting down covered in it, and he was
just staring at my tackle.

**Parry**  He probably fancied you. I've heard he likes a big strong Yorkie
Bar.

**Mick**  What?

**Parry**  I never let him near me.

**Mick**  He had his hands all over me. He shaved me for the operation.

**POM**  Me too.

**Mick**  I thought he was taking his time when he shaved my pubes.

**Parry**  Probably made his day.

**Mick**  Fucking hell! I'll have him!

**Parry**  I didn't think he was your type, Michael!

*Mick rushes out followed by Parry*

*Ian laughs at POM*

*Black-out*

*2.30 a.m. The next morning*

*The Lights come up very dimly*

*Ian, Keith and POM are in their beds, asleep*

**Ian** (*talking in his sleep more fluently than when conscious*) Where's the OP? Look in the webbing. No. I told you I left it with ... Tango Charlie to Charlie One. Did he say he'd call back or should we go to the OP?

*There is a pause*

**POM** (*talking in his sleep*) Wait for me under the bridge.

*Another pause*

**Ian** Tango Charlie, Tango Charlie, we can't stay here any longer. Too exposed. Must move to cover.
**POM** (*laughing*) Yeah — bring him with you, he'll only squeal.
**Ian** Is it safe?
**POM** Keep near the river bed.
**Ian** It's not safe.
**POM** Don't know.
**Ian** Not safe.
**POM** I don't know.
**Ian** Not safe.
**POM** Don't know.
**Keith** (*sitting up*) Will youse both go back to base. Mission abandoned. You're relieved from the operation. (*Beat*) Jesus, we'll all be relieved.

*There is a pause. During the following, POM looks round at Keith and Ian*

**Ian** (*distressed, sitting bolt upright*) Sunray down. Repeat. Sunray down. Three, possibly four players. Unidentified. I can't see them. Can't see them. Sunray down. Head ... his head's gone. (*He scratches the scar on his temple, then starts to shake and sob*)
**Keith** (*getting out of bed and going to Ian*) It's OK, it's OK. Come on now. (*He helps Ian back to sleep*) Ssh. Ssh. Here we go. Snug as a bug in a — (*Noticing POM; to him*) Are you awake? (*He crosses over to POM's bed to get a better look at him and realizes that POM is really still asleep, and won't remember what has happened when he wakes up in the morning*) Go back to sleep sir. (*He gets back into bed*)

*Just as Keith settles, Joe sneaks into the bay, holding his shoes*

What time do you call this?

**Joe** Fuck me! What are you doing up?

**Keith** Ian's found a soul mate.

**Joe** Not him as well.

**Keith** You should hear him. He's leading the fucking D-Day landings he is.

**Joe** Why do we always get the screamers? (*He gets undressed during the following*) Hey, it's a beautiful night out there you know Keith. They've cut the grass on the way to the *Tuns*. I love the smell of cut grass. I wish you could get out there and see it.

**Keith** I thought you were going to be back for the game. Four-three. You missed a cracker.

**Joe** Eh! Fuck off. It was one-all.

**Keith** Who told you?

**Joe** I saw it, didn't I?

**Keith** They haven't got a telly in the *Tuns*.

**Joe** I know.

**Keith** So?

**Joe** Wouldn't you like to know. (*Beat*) I got a better offer.

**Keith** What do you mean you got a better offer?

**Joe** Well, she's brunette, great tits, lovely body altogether actually.

*Keith gets out of bed, checks the corridor, then hops over and sits on Joe's bed. He pats the bed. Joe is still putting his clothes away*

**Keith** Who?

**Joe** Gillian. Well ... Gill.

**Keith** Gillian who?

**Joe** She came in this afternoon apparently. Ingrowing toenails. (*Either naked or just in his underpants, he gets into bed*) The major's wife in the room at the end.

**Keith** (*laughing*) No. Who is it really? You're winding me up.

**Joe** We just sparked. You know how you can do that sometimes.

**Keith** Sparked! There are going to be sparks all right.

**Joe** We just got chatting, and one thing led to another. It was a bit frustrating with her foot bandaged up. And my finger. (*He looks at his own bandaged hand, with the third finger missing*) I'm really going to miss that finger you know.

**Keith** A major's wife!

**Joe** I used to do all my preparatory work with that finger.

**Keith** Shit! I'm implicated now. Why did you have to tell me?

**Joe** I told you because you're the only person I could tell. I thought you were my mate. (*Beat*) So if you don't like it Keith ——
**POM** How much? Nine thousand! I can't. No, no, no, no, no.
**Joe** (*raising his voice*) Shut up.
**POM** It's OK.
**Joe** Good-night Keith.


SCENE 3

*Afternoon. A few days later*

*Under the scene change we hear the soundtrack of an old Tom and Jerry cartoon, with lots of crashes and bangs. The Lights come up. The cartoon soundtrack fades on the theatre speakers so that it is coming from the TV alone. This fades during the opening dialogue*

*Keith and Joe are sitting up on Keith's bed like Mummy and Daddy holding court. POM is lying on his bed. Mick and Parry are sitting near Keith's bed. They are reading contact magazines. Mick has a notebook and pen. Ian is watching TV but listening to the conversation. POM is rather left out of the conversation*

**Joe** Here we go. (*Reading*) "Leggy blonde 36-25-38 desires well-endowed man for sexy evenings."
**Parry** Let's have a look. Is there a piccy?
**Mick** What's the reference? (*Writing*) How old?
**Joe** Late thirties. "Voyeur husband with approval would participate." T43.
**Mick** I knew this would happen. You always have to go over the edge.
**Joe** We're not.
**Keith** We're just trying to help you find the woman of your dreams.
**Mick** This is a waste of time. I'm not going to find a warm, satisfying relationship in any of this porn.
**Joe** It's not porn. They're contact magazines for swinging adults.
**Keith** Mickey, you opened your wee little heart to us, and we appreciated that.
**Parry** Course we did.
**Keith** So we just want to help you find that someone special who can enjoy the new you.
**POM** What about *Time Out*? There's a lonely hearts in the back of *Time Out*.
**Mick** Oh yeah, right.
**Joe** I found a really nice divorcee in this one just after I came out that second time.

**Keith** It was probably because of her that they had to re-admit him.

**Joe** Her husband ran off with a younger man.

**Parry** You what?

**Mick** That's disgusting.

**Joe** She was well horny enough. Had a beautiful chassis for her age. But she was all screwed-up about her husband turning ringer.

**Parry** I prefer older women.

**Joe** I couldn't satisfy her though. Well, I was a sick man.

**Keith** Excuse me I thought I heard the "Battersea Boner" say there was a female he couldn't satisfy!

**Joe** To tell the truth. I said to myself "Joe, you're not a milking machine." I wanted to be appreciated for my personality — not how much I could make her come.

**Parry** I first did it when I was thirteen.

**Keith** And when did we get on to this topic of conversation?

**Parry** Porked the baby-sitter, Janet, during Match of the Day! I scored more than West Ham that night! In fact I've been told I've got the looks that older women go for. They want to look after me because I look vulnerable.

**Keith** You look about as vulnerable as a self-loading fucking rifle!

**Joe** What about this one? (*Pretending to read*) "Voluptuous yet sensitive, caring, shy but very randy young oriental lady —— "

**Mick** She could be the one ...

**Joe** " — is looking for the man of her fantasies. Must be a member of Her Majesty's Armed Forces, preferably a squaddy in the Artillery who has just been circumcised. Hopefully his name will be Gunner Michael Speedy, because I want him to shoot his load as fast as possible!"

**Mick** Fuck off!

**Parry** Oriental women. Lovely. Me and this mate from the Coldstream — that's your mob isn't it sir? Yeah, 2nd Battalion he was — we had a forty-eight hourer in Bangkok, and we went to this parlour called "Wonkee Dicks".

*Keith and Joe start to snore*

Straight up. Shut up! Listen. They lined all the girls up and you chose the one you wanted, then after the massage she asks if you want any extras — "fucky or blowey" — and they've got this special trick, right: when you start coming she sticks her middle finger right up your arse and twiddles something so that you can't stop coming. I thought I'd died and gone to heaven.

**Mick** (*after a pause*) How do you know it was her middle finger?

**Keith** They're only kids, you know that.

**Parry** I like them young. Less chance of disease then.

**Keith** They're kids and they're forced into it. They're sold off to feed their parents' heroin addiction. You better get yourself checked out.

*POM starts to walk away from his bed*

   (*To POM*) And you, you're on bed rest.
**POM** I was just ——
**Keith** Get back on your bed.
**Joe** (*deflecting the tension*) So, what are we left with? Three definites, two possibilities, one, two, three, four extremely unlikelies but have a go anyway, and two "I like them and don't care what the others think."
**Mick** I said they were ——
**Joe** Be fair, it was only the handicapped one we threw out.
**Keith** And that's because we thought they'd have too much in common.
**Parry** Eh! What about us then, Ian? We'd do brilliant on the sympathy front. We'd have to fight them off, Ian. "Northern Ireland veterans. One shot in the head but getting better, seek that extra special Florence Nightingale to help with feeding, bed wetting, and nasty nightmares ... "
**Joe** Parry!
**Mick** Easy Parry.
**Parry** What about me then? "Falklands veteran —— "
**Keith** Uh uh, you didn't go down there.
**Parry** Yeah, but they ain't going to know that are they? All right then, "Irresistible Fusilier. Northern Ireland veteran. Wounded and decorated —— "
**Joe** Fucking painted and decorated.
**Parry** "—will satisfy any woman — older housewives especially welcome."
**Keith** Fusilier? They won't know what a Fusilier is.
**Mick** Nobody knows what a Fusilier is.
**Parry** All right, Commando.
**Keith** Commando! Infantry grunt.
**Parry** That Major's wife knew what a Fusilier was all right. I'm sure she was giving me the eye this morning outside the toilet.

*Keith looks at Joe*

**Joe** I don't think so Parry.
**Mick** Nah. You don't want to get involved with any of that Parry. That's playing with fire that is.
**Keith** Too right ——
**Joe** Now Mick have you got the photos?
**Mick** What for?
**Joe** To send off with your letters.

**Mick** What letters?

**Joe** Are you sure you're in Intelligence?

**Mick** I'm not. I'm Artillery.

**Joe** I know. It was a fucking joke, you gun bunny.

**Mick** Look hold on. This isn't what I wanted. I want something more serious.

**Joe** Serious — what do you mean, serious?

**Mick** I want someone I can talk to.

**Joe** Why?

**Parry** No. Be fair. Mick's got a point. My dad was a Fusilier and his dad before him, and he always used to say there are those you marry and then there are those you have a good time with, and don't get them confused.

**Keith** That explains it. A family of fucking grunts!

**Joe** You're better off with a wife who knows what it's about. If her dad's a soldier she'll have it in her blood.

**Mick** I didn't mean that. I didn't mean ... I want it to be different. I don't want that. (*He picks up the copy of* Time Out *on POM's cabinet*)

*During the following, POM shows Mick the back pages of* Time Out *where the Lonely Hearts column can be found, and Mick studies it*

**Parry** Look at that. "Will pose for anything legal"! Anyone know where I can get a cheap second-hand 35 millimetre?

**Joe** Yours not working either? I didn't know it was that small.

**Parry** No. I've only got an Instamatic. (*Then he gets the joke*) Fuck off! No-one's ever complained about my packed lunch. I can't turn up to take erotic portraits with a fucking Kodak Instamatic.

**Joe** Course you can.

**Parry** How could I get the films developed? It's illegal.

**Joe** You can send them away. There's special laboratories.

**POM** What about a Polaroid?

**Parry** Of course. A Polaroid! How much do you reckon they are then? (*He gets out his wallet*)

**Joe** Oh hallo. You'll have to dust the cobwebs off that.

**Keith** Christ! Take cover. A grunt with a loaded wallet.

**Parry** Are you trying to imply something?

*During the following, Joe collects up all the contact magazines and stuffs them under his pillow*

**Joe** Imply? You are joking. Parry, you are always on the fucking scrounge.

**Keith** Moses had less trouble parting the Dead Sea than you opening your wallet.

**Parry** Fuck off! I'm not tight.

**Joe** Oh good. Well, you can pay for the photos then.

**Parry** What?

**Joe** We're all going to hold Mick's hand. The excitement. It might all be too much. He might split his stitches.

**Parry** Hold on.

**Keith** What do you reckon then? Should he have them done bare-chested, pyjama top or dressing-gown?

**Joe** Decisions, decisions.

**Mick** Hey lads (*reading from* Time Out) — what's a "Vegan"? (*Which he mispronounces to rhyme with Megan*)

**Keith** We won't be long, sir.

**Parry** Oi. Hold on. I haven't got any change. It takes fifties and I haven't got any change.

**Joe** Oh that's a surprise isn't it Parry! You got any fifties?

**Keith** No I'm right out of fifties at the moment.

**Joe** What about you?

**Mick** No I ain't got none.

**Joe** So, we're short of fifties then?

**Keith** Yeah. No fifties at all.

**Mick** Oh yeah. No fifties at all.

**POM** Hold on. I've probably got one. Lots of loose change for the phone. Yes, here we are. (*He produces a bag of change and offers Joe a fifty pence piece*)

**Joe** (*taking the whole bag of change*) Why don't you come with us? We can get a few with us lot together. And on the way you can tell us about when you lost your cherry.

**POM** You wouldn't believe it.

**Joe** You did mention something about a horse in your sleep last night.

**POM** Whoops. Given it away. What about my bed rest?

*Parry, Mick and Keith move into the corridor, heading for the exit, Joe and POM following them during the coming dialogue. POM is terribly worried that his bag of change, which is his lifeline to the outside world, has been taken. He can't take his eyes off it*

**Joe** (*stepping into the corridor*) Just this once. You can treat us all to a brew off the Naafi wagon.

*Parry is by now almost out of view*

(*To Parry*) And you, Parry, bring your fucking smokes — I'm fed up of you poncing mine.

**POM** (*stepping into the corridor*) I will need a couple of those fifties for the phone.

*They all exit, leaving Ian*

*Ian waits for them to go, then wheels himself over to Joe's bed. He pushes the pillow to one side to reveal one of the magazines. He opens it at a photo of a naked woman. He stares at this but angrily closes the magazine and manoeuvres it back under the pillow. He sits staring at the pillow as the Lights fade to Black-out*

SCENE 4

*Early afternoon. A few days later*

*The Lights come up*

*Only Ian and Keith are on stage. Ian is exercising his arms by pushing his torso up out of his wheelchair and down again. Keith is listening to his personal stereo while playing chess, with half an eye on Ian*

*Ian pushes himself up with great effort three or four times before:*

*Joe enters carrying a plastic carrier bag from which he gets out a brown paper bag of fruit and a cake box. He hides the cake box under his bed and puts the fruit in a bowl on Ian's bedside cabinet. Joe watches Ian for a few moments, then turns to Keith*

**Joe**  How many has he done now?
**Keith**  (*shouting*) Eh?
**Joe**  I said how many?
**Keith**  About twenty-five, thirty.
**Joe**  No need to shout.
**Keith**  What?
**Joe**  That's brilliant, Ian. Did you keep count for Sheila how many you've done?

*Ian nods*

How many did you do? Ian? Was it thirty?
**Ian**  (*as he pushes up again with great determination*) Six.
**Joe**  Six! Keith said you'd done nearly thirty.
**Ian**  Hundred and six. Hundred and seven.
**Joe**  Didn't Keith tell you to stop at fifty? Whoa whoa whoa, take it easy. That's too much Ian. What else did you do in physio today?
**Ian**  (*putting a finger up his nose*) Good for fingers.

**Joe**  What about neck rolls?

*Ian starts to move his head in a slow neck roll with his finger still up his nose*

**Keith**  (*still shouting*) How about that for co-ordination?
**Joe**  Why didn't you tell him to stop at fifty?
**Keith**  I can't hear you.
**Joe**  Why didn't you tell him to stop at fifty?
**Keith**  Why stop at fifty? I'm not his mother.
**Joe**  (*going to Keith*) I've got it sorted.
**Keith**  Eh? (*He takes his headphones off*) What?
**Joe**  I've been to the bakers.
**Keith**  (*sarcastically*) Good.
**Joe**  (*after a pause*) I'm sorry about the snooker.
**Keith**  Forget it.
**Joe**  I'm sorry Keith.
**Keith**  I played a few frames with the Rupert.
**Joe**  Shall I book the table for tomorrow?
**Keith**  Whatever.
**Joe**  Can he play?
**Keith**  Yeah, he's not bad. He potted a few.
**Joe**  Did you win?
**Keith**  Look we only played a couple of frames because I was waiting on you.
**Joe**  It took longer than I thought.
**Keith**  Did you show Gilly the cake then?
**Joe**  What?
**Keith**  On your way back. I saw you coming.
**Joe**  I just popped in.
**Keith**  You should be more careful then, shouldn't you?

*Joe overreacts by shouting at Keith. This is a symptom of his post-traumatic stress*

**Joe**  I didn't see the time! (*He pauses, regaining his composure*) I'll go and book it for tomorrow then yeah? When's the best time for you.
**Keith**  Well, you're the one with the busy schedule. (*He puts his headphones on again*)

*Joe walks back to his own bed. He stands there for a moment then violently kicks his table and exits*

*POM enters, passing Joe in the corridor. POM has his bag of change and his address book with him*

**POM**  Bad as a fruit machine that phone. (*He starts eating his apple*)
**Ian**  Keith. Keith. (*Louder*) Leak please Keith.
**POM**  Keith! I think he needs the loo.
**Keith**  What? (*He takes his headphones off*)
**POM**  He needs the toilet.
**Ian**  Leak.
**Keith**  Jesus Christ! Why didn't you say so a minute ago. (*He picks up a cardboard bedpan and moves to Ian — but he sees that Ian has already wet himself*) Oh Christ, Ian. Looks like we missed it again. Must be all this aerobics. Don't you worry, my old son.

*Keith puts Ian's feet back on the rest plates and wheels Ian towards the exit*

Penny for the guy. Penny for the guy.

*They exit*

**Ian**  (*off*) Shut up!

*POM follows them off*

*Mick enters with a letter*

**Mick**  Hey lads, guess what I've been sent. You'll never guess what I just got. (*He realizes the others have all gone*) Shit! (*He smells the envelope, then opens it; reading*) "Dear Michael, or would you prefer Mike?" (*He ponders for a moment then shrugs, mouthing "Whatever" to himself*) "Enjoyed reading your letter. Had over a thousand replies." A thousand replies! "But feel you could be that someone special I am looking for. Always wanted to meet a Gunner. Hope you like the photo ... Was yours taken in a photo booth, ha ha?" Photo-booth-ha-ha?! Oh! Photo booth. Ha ha! Oh yes. (*He laughs*) "I hope the operation was a success." (*He looks at the photo*) Yes. Fucking hell you could be the one. And you're gorgeous! The lads aren't going to believe this. (*He kisses the photo*) Stop. Ah. Stop. Ice. Ice, ice, ice. Mrs Thatcher, Mrs Thatcher, Mrs Thatcher. Sitting on blocks of ice. (*Beat*) With Mrs Thatcher. (*He then carefully lifts up the waist band of his jogging pants to check his stitches*) "I'm looking for Mr Right. Could he be Gunner Right? Who'd talk to me a lot, and not just dirty." What? "Awaiting your reply with wet anticipation, Una." (*He thinks*) Always wanted

to meet a Gunner. Photo booth. (*He looks at the envelope*) Posted in
Woolwich! You bastards. I knew it was too soon.

*Black-out*


SCENE 5

*Late afternoon. Some days later*

*The Lights come up*

*POM lies on his bed reading* The Wasp Factory

*Keith enters, close to tears*

**Keith**  For fuck's sake. The fuckers. Sly fuckers. "Is our pain mental,
not physical?" I frigging ask you! This four-eyed frog of a captain says
(*imitating the Captain*) "Did we fink our leg might be caused by a vewy
intense psychological twauma? Are we sure it isn't mental?" I've been
in this place for a year, all the pain and the tests and now they come up
with this mullarky. I said "The reason we know it's not mental, sir, is
because our fucking leg hurts. It throbs. It causes us pain."

*Silence*

**POM**  I'm sorry.
**Keith**  Thirteen months and all they can come up with is that. (*He pauses*)
They've notched up another one — (*He lifts the leg of his shorts and
shows POM the new line drawn on his upper thigh*)
**POM**  Those lines ——
**Keith**  — so I don't know what they're playing at.
**POM**  What are they for?
**Keith**  That's how they keep track of the numbness. Every few months
they notch up another one, a bit higher up. A bit more that I can't feel.
**POM**  What actually happened?
**Keith**  I went on a run one day and it seized up. I thought it was cramp
to begin with, but you don't have cramp creeping up your leg for over
a year, do you?
**POM**  They'll know what it is.
**Keith**  No, they don't.
**POM**  They seem pretty good here. I'm sure they'll have some idea.
**Keith**  (*shouting at POM*) I just said they don't. (*He pauses*) What are
you reading then, sir?

**POM** *The Wasp Factory.*
**Keith** *The Wasp Factory?*
**POM** Yes.
**Keith** About wasps is it?
**POM** No, not really.
**Keith** A factory?
**POM** No.
**Keith** Why is it called *The Wasp Factory* then if it's not about wasps or a factory?
**POM** Well, it is in a way I suppose.
**Keith** Ah! One of those kind of books.

*There is a pause. Keith makes himself comfortable on his bed*

My father kept bees.
**POM** Oh?
**Keith** Ay. But he died. Killed. (*Beat*) He was a superintendent in the RUC. '71 it was. He kept bees though. My ma's remarried. My stepfather's in the RUC. (*Beat*) My ma was very lucky. It was an IRA gunman, in a mask. Burst into the house. Shot him in bed. I didn't hear any of it though — slept through it all.
**POM** Why did you want to join the Army?
**Keith** I was unemployed. Unemployable, my ma said. I didn't do too well at school you see. I'm more your practical get-up-and-do-it sort of person. We can't all get lots of qualifications and go to university.
**POM** Why do you assume I've got lots of qualifications and been to university?
**Keith** Because you read books with titles like *The Wasp Factory*. (*He pauses*) I don't know, the more qualifications your lot seem to have the more stupid they are. No common sense. You'll find that out sir. Take Parry — now he's the victim of a berk of a Rupert if you don't mind me saying so.
**POM** No. Go on.
**Keith** He was on a night patrol with a young Rupert who'd just finished college and couldn't map-read. The patrol ends up spending most of the night up to their necks in a river rather than this Rupert admitting he couldn't hack it. When they do finally get back to their bivvis Parry's put on the first two hour stag. He asks the Rupert if he can change his wet socks but the Rupert tells him not to be a wimp. They found him the next morning collapsed with frostbite. They had to cut his boots away from his feet. So off with the toes. He was lucky they managed to save the big ones. At least he'll have some balance left. The Rupert gets off with a slapped wrist and a map-reading course.
**POM** Christ.

*Silence*

Why do you call officers Ruperts?

**Keith** (*thinking*) I don't know. Why do you call officers Ruperts?

**POM** No. I mean where does it come from?

**Keith** Maybe it's got something to do with them all being called Rodney and Rupert.

**POM** But it's not really like that any more. Is it?

**Keith** Isn't it? My platoon commander was called Archibald Lightfoot. Archibald "Haggis" Lightfoot.Why did you join the Army? You don't quite seem the type.

**POM** Oh ... Um. Doesn't matter.

**Keith** Sorry sir. Overstepped the mark there didn't we Keith.

**POM** No. That's not ... It's complicated. (*He pauses*) Fancy another frame or two later? I think I've cracked it with the old vertical cueing action.

**Keith** It probably won't be free. You have to book.

**POM** Is everything ready?

**Keith** Ay. All set. Just waiting on Joe. And for the birthday boy to finish with the physio terrorists.

**POM** What are you listening to?

**Keith** The King.

**POM** Elvis.

**Keith** Meatloaf. Oh Christ! A herd of grunts!

*Parry enters with Mick. Parry has six party hats and a box of party poppers in his lap; Mick has with him a huge birthday card in its envelope*

**Parry** Take them off. Take them off. I've got a cracker for you. What's the difference between dead people and boomerangs?

**Mick** Dead people don't ... (*He laughs*)

**Parry** Shut up. What's the difference? You're supposed to laugh. Don't you get it? He got it for fuck's sake. Because then I say oh you've heard it. Because it's obvious isn't it?

**Mick** Yeah, it's obvious. (*He stops laughing, looking at Keith and POM*)

*Keith and POM are stony-faced*

**Parry** Dead people don't come back!

**Mick** Actually Parry I still don't get it.

**Keith** Parry.

**Parry** What?

**Keith** Have you ever thought of a career in comedy?

**Parry** Fuck off! My humour's just too quick for the Irish Rangers. (*He throws Keith a party hat*) All the same, you Paddies. Thick as pig shit.
**Keith** I'd watch it if I was you.
**Parry** Yeah?
**Mick** Are we all set then?
**POM** Yes. Just waiting for Ian to come back from physio.
**Mick** Where's Joe?
**POM** Yes, where is Joe?
**Mick** He is coming, isn't he?
**Keith** Ay. I'll bet he is.
**Mick** What? 'Cause he's got all the gear hasn't he? I've got the card. (*He gets out the huge card*) Thought we'd give him a nice big one for the old two one.
**POM** Good Lord.
**Mick** Yeah. Impressive isn't it?
**Keith** Mick, it's disgusting.
**Mick** Are there two t's in congratulations? (*He writes in the card*)
**Keith** What do you think?

*Joe enters hurriedly with the tea things on a tray; they include the cake, with candles, and a cake knife*

**Joe** Right then. How we doing?
**Keith** We've been waiting on you.
**Joe** It's all under control. I've just been getting this lot together. (*He gets the present out of his cabinet*)
**Mick** There we go. Now if we can all sign it. (*He passes the card to Keith*)
**Keith** Congratulations on your ... (*Beat*) For fuck's sake, Mick! Congratulations hasn't got double "t". (*He gives the card to POM*) Has it?
**POM** No. One "t" in congratulations. (*He signs the card*)
**Keith** Why didn't you ask if you didn't know?
**Mick** I did ask.
**Keith** When?
**Mick** Just now. I said "Has congratulations got two t's?" and you said "What do you think?" and that's what I thought. It's not my fault, is it Joe?
**Keith** Whose fault is it, then?
**POM** I don't think it really matters. Who's going to notice? (*He hands the card to Joe*)

*During the following, Joe lights the cake candles and signs the card*

**Keith** I did.
**Mick** Well I'm sorry.

**Keith**  At least we've solved the problem of what to get you on your
birthday — a fucking dictionary!

*Ian appears in the corridor*

**Parry**  (*noticing Ian*) Ay ay.

*Ian enters the bay. This catches the others unprepared They start singing
"Happy Birthday to you", and Joe surreptitiously puts the card in the
envelope. They all put their party hats on. Ian isn't aware that the party
celebrations are for him until he hears his name. Keith puts a party hat
on Ian. All the hats are different but Mick's should be in the shape of a
pirate captain's hat with skull and crossbones on it*

**Joe**  (*reading from a piece of paper*) On behalf of all the boys — oh, and
Mr Menzies — I'll raise my voice above the noise to wish a very special
mate on this a very special date a very happy 21st. So raise your cup and
give three cheers (*he whispers*) 'cause after tea we've got some beers!
**Keith**  Thank you Lord Byron!
**Parry**  Poppers!

*All except Ian take a party popper out of the box that Parry is holding.
They point the poppers at Ian like a firing squad*

**Joe**  (*as a military command*) Present poppers! Fire!

*The poppers go off with a loud bang which makes Ian jump*

No, seriously, three months in a coma probably seems a doddle
compared to a few weeks with us. And we just wanted to say in our
own little way many happy returns. (*He gives Ian the card*)
**Mick**  Bumps?

*Joe gets the present out*

**Parry**  Speech, speech.
**Ian**  Is this a wind-up?
**POM**  More of a blow-up actually.
**Joe**  (*as Jimmy Savile*) "Now then, now then: was that really you up
there on that there ladder Dr Destruction, ho ho. No Green of the
goodly Jackets should be without one of these!" (*As himself*) Go on,
open it then.
**Parry**  Better than any girlfriend except it can't squeeze your blackheads
for you.

**Keith** You know Parry, you've got a real way with women, haven't you?
**Mick** We can help you choose a name.
**Joe** Let's have some element of surprise for fuck's sake!

*Ian unwraps the present and looks at the doll*

**Parry** I might have to borrow her off you.
**Keith** Take her home to meet the parents?
**Ian** Stop it.

*Silence*

**Joe** It was only a joke.

*Silence*

**Ian** Can't.
**Joe** What?
**Ian** Can't ... (*He throws the doll and the box to the floor*)
**Mick** I think he means he can't ——
**Joe** Yes all right, we've gathered that. (*He pauses*) I was impotent for nearly a year after. It's just a question of time.
**POM** Yes, it's just a temporary thing isn't it? I'm sure it'll clear up.
**Keith** Well, Bay 4, we've really hit the jackpot this time.
**Parry** We didn't know. How could we have ——
**Joe** We could have known. I'm sorry Ian.

*There is a pause. Ian is unforgiving*

(*Picking up the doll and the box and putting them on his bed*) Who's for tea, then?
**Mick** And cake?

*Joe pours the tea. POM pours the milk. Joe takes a cup of tea to Ian and puts his "curly wurly" straw in the cup. After all the teas have been poured Joe gets the knife*

**Joe** (*deadpan*) Right. Fall in for cake. (*He cuts the cake*)

*They all gather round to get cake then disperse around the room in embarrassed silence. It is important for the comedy of the following sequence that Parry should end up furthest upstage and c, the others not paying him any particular attention. Ian sits in his wheelchair by his own bed with his back to the others and with the birthday card on his lap. Joe puts a piece of cake in Ian's hand. They all sit in silence eating the cake. The longer the silence the better! Although it will be Parry who will determine this*

**Parry** (*floating it in to the air*) Here Mick?
**Mick** What?
**Parry** You had any more letters lately?

*Parry, POM, Keith and Joe burst out laughing — Ian and Mick do not*

**Mick** (*turning away*) Bunch of twats.

*This makes the others laugh even more*

   (*Taking a bite of his cake and speaking with his mouth full*) Magic cake Ian.
**POM** (*taking a sip of his tea*) And you can't beat the Count Brown.
**Keith** The what?
**POM** The Count Brown. When I was a child we always called the Earl Grey tea that my Nanna made the Count Brown.
**Mick** Oh what! I wanted proper tea.
**Parry** Nanna? What kind of name is that?
**POM** We always called my grandmother Nanna.
**Keith** Nanna! Nanna! I suppose it's Mummy and Daddy as well. (*Mimicking*) "Oh Mummy, Nanna made us some super Count Brown." "Did she, darling precious pumpkin?"
**POM** What do you call your grandmother?
**Keith** Surprisingly enough I call her Grandma. I have been known to call her Granny. But she definitely draws the line at Nanna!
**POM** That's just as bad. What about you Parry?
**Parry** I haven't got any. They're all dead.
**Keith** "And our survey said? ... "
**Keith**  ⎫
**Joe**    ⎬ (*together*) "Ugh ugh!" (*This is a catch phrase from the popular*
**Parry**  ⎭       *TV game show* Family Fortunes)
**Mick** We always called our Grandma "Grunks" and Grandpa "Grandie".
**POM** That's what we called our grandfather.
**Keith** Oh, Mickey, how absolutely spiffing. I really do wonder about you sir. Most of the time you seem quite normal.
**Mick** I remember when I was a kid there were things I couldn't pronounce properly — like bacon and eggs was always "Naconeggs".
**POM** I used to love fried eggs on marmaladed toast — that was always "Neggstoastmamjam".

*There is a stunned silence*

**Joe** You like fried eggs on marmaladed toast?
**POM** You ever tried it?
**Joe** No I have not.
**Mick** What else couldn't I say?
**Keith** Foreskin, circumcision?
**Parry** Fuck off?
**Mick** Fuck off!
**Parry** Definite improvement with that one!
**Joe** It would seem that Mr Menzies and Captain Pugwash have got rather a lot in common. Definite Potential Officer material wouldn't you say sir?
**Mick** All right then. (*He gets up out of his wheelchair, legs wide apart, holding his trousers away from his genitalia*)
**Joe** Oi oi.
**Keith** Steady.
**Joe** Watch your midships!
**Mick** What if I was to tell you that I had recently applied for a Potential Officer's course?

*The others burst out laughing*

Go on then. Go on. He who laughs last laughs loudest.
**Joe** Longest!
**Mick** And longest.
**Ian** (*laughing, shouting to be heard*) It's not my birthday.

*The others laugh even more*

It's not my birthday today.

*Silence*

**Joe** What do you mean it's not your birthday today?
**Keith** When is it? Tomorrow?
**Ian** June. (*He laughs again*)
**Parry** What?
**Keith** What do you mean it's June?
**Mick** Ian, this is March, don't you mean March?
**Joe** What date?
**Mick** This is March isn't it?
**Ian** 3rd of June. Three. Six. Six. Three. (*He laughs*)
**Keith** You know what's happened don't you? I don't believe this.

**Mick**  Oh fuck!

**Keith**  Oh yes, quite a large fuck I'm afraid. It's the 6th of the 3rd. Thank you Sheila. She's got the dates the wrong way round.

**Parry**  Typical fucking female. (*He takes his party hat off*)

**Joe**  Why didn't you think to check?

**Keith**  Me? So it's my fault now is it?

**Joe**  Did Sheila actually say his birthday was today?

**Parry**  Well I heard her talking about it.

**Joe**  Did she say it's Ian's birthday on the 6th of March?

**POM**  Didn't anyone think of checking his wrist band? Date of birth is on that.

**Joe**  Why didn't you think to check? You're the fucking officer!

**POM**  (*taking in what Joe has said to him*) What? What did you say? What have I done that merits this "you're the officer" bit? I'm not even that. It's *Potential* Officer, remember? You've always been quick to point that one out. And if you want to know the truth I don't particularly give a fuck about the whole fucking thing anyway. I didn't want to be moved here as much as you didn't want me, and as it has so often been pointed out to me I'll only be here for another week or so anyway. (*He waddles towards the exit, desperately trying to keep his dignity. He stops in the doorway*) Oh, and if I am an officer we may as well stick to formalities as I seem to offend you so much as a person.

*He exits*

**Parry**  Fucking hell! What brought that on?

**Mick**  I suppose he thought it was his fault — getting the dates wrong. We weren't blaming him though, were we?

**Keith**  I don't blame him. I just don't like officers!

**Mick**  He's all right. Doesn't seem the dangerous type. I think he'd make a good Rupert.

**Joe**  (*sitting on POM's bed*) Do you reckon the Ruperts know we're in charge really?

**Parry**  Eh?

**Keith**  No. It goes to their heads.

**Parry**  What about the "Brass"?

**Joe**  I'm talking about on the ground where it counts. The sharp end. But it's always been like that. Hasn't it? They're the leaders but we do the leading. The NCO's I mean.

**Mick**  Someone thought he'd be a suitable officer. Regular Commissions Board.

**Joe**  No. I found out he was an Army Scholar.

**Mick**  An Army Scholar?

**Joe**  Through the back door.

**Parry** How's that then?

**Joe** In at sixteen, a few interviews and Bob's your uncle, or your Nanna! A place at Sandhurst and two years of dosh while you finish school — then another three years of dosh for college so that you can get those all-important exams which of course make you that better an officer.

**Mick** Some people are dead jammy.

**Parry** I went in at sixteen and no one gave me any money.

**Joe** Yeah, but you're not exactly an investment are you?

**Parry** I think I am.

**Keith** Junior Leaders is meant to keep thugs like you off the streets.

**Mick** My mum thinks I'm an investment.

**Joe** What! Yeah, but I'm afraid your mum isn't in charge of giving out Army Scholarships, is she? It's not just them, we all do it. It's part of the game.

**Mick** What game?

**Joe** This. The whole thing. The Army. Life. I don't know.

**Parry** Fucking hell, what's your problem?

**Mick** I certainly don't see the Army as a game. I see it as a very serious business. You've been in here too long if you think that.

**Joe** All right then — after that patrol why didn't you just go and change your wet socks? You could have done it quietly, no questions asked. But no, you obeyed a command even though you knew the Rupert was a liability and you end up with them cutting blocks of ice away from your feet.

**Parry** I don't know. You just do, don't you?

**Joe** Course you know. You're choosing not to.

**Parry** All right, well it's the training isn't it? It's the rules.

**Joe** Exactly. The rules of the game.

**Parry** You ain't any better than us.

**Joe** Maybe not, but at least I'm beginning to realize I've got one of these (*he points to his head*) and it does work by itself.

**Keith** Come on Joe. We all do it, game or no game. If you start deciding which orders to obey and which ones not to then you're fucked. You know it's not Queen and Country — you do it for your mates.

**Mick** It's no game patrolling the Falls Road: ask Ian.

**Keith** Everyone has to be on the same wavelength. No weak links, remember? At the end of the day you have to trust they know what they're doing?

**Joe** But who's they? Them or us? You've changed your tune haven't you? So now, Keithy, you trust them to find out what's wrong with your leg do you?

**Keith** That's different.

**Joe** You've been in here a year for fuck's sake. Is it physical Keith? Why can't they find out what's wrong? Is it your leg or is it up here?

(*He points to his head*) Are you sure they aren't trying to make you fit into their nice little diagnosis because there's no fucking room for something they can't understand? Nine times out of ten they're lucky or they may even get it right but you're number ten. The exception that proves the fucking rule.

**Parry**  You ain't a doctor Joe.

**Keith**  They're doctors before they're soldiers.

**Joe**  Who really gives a fuck about us anyway? I don't see any of them leaping to find a fucking answer. We're not important enough. They probably want to keep me here because they know I'm a good story, and they can wheel me out every once in a while. But you're not even that are you?

**Keith**  They sent your finger to be analysed in America. It was a very rare blood infection.

**Joe**  They could have sent me too.

**Keith**  It was going to have to come off sooner or later.

**Joe**  I would have preferred later. And why haven't they got the facilities here? We only have their word for it that it had to come off in the first place. I hope you feel the same way when they take your fucking leg off!

**Ian**  Stop it! Don't argue! Don't do this. Just stop it. (*He takes his party hat off*)

*Silence. Joe and Keith go back to their respective beds*

**Parry**  Let's unpack a pack, eh?

**Joe**  Yeah. All right, go on.

*Parry gets some beers out of Joe's cabinet. He gives a four-pack to Joe. Joe passes a can to Ian then goes to give one to Keith by way of making up*

**Mick**  Save some for Mr Menzies?

**Parry**  Hark at him. Now he knows the Rupert got an Army Scholarship he wants to make a little nest up his bum!

**Mick**  No I don't.

**Joe**  What do you think Ian, shall we save some for the PO?

**Ian**  Yeah, let's get him pissed.

**Parry**  There is of course the small matter of Titania. (*He gets out the doll and starts to blow it up*)

**Mick**  Who?

**Parry**  Fucking hell, has anyone got a pump? (*He continues blowing up the doll*)

**Mick**  Titania! She doesn't look like a ...

*There is a silence. Parry stops*

*POM enters and lies on his bed*

*The others hide their cans of beer under their clothing. POM picks up*
*Mick's party hat from his bedside cabinet and drops it on the floor. He*
*resumes reading* The Wasp Factory

**Joe**  Would you like a beer sir?
**POM**  No thank you.
**Mick**  Go on sir.
**POM**  I said no.

*Ian wheels himself over to POM's bed and puts his can of lager on*
*POM's table*

Thank you. (*He stares at the can*) Cheers! (*He takes the can*) The
others immediately get out their cans and pull the ring-pulls
**Parry**  Result!
**POM**  (*looking round and realizing the others had cans of beer all*
*along*) Listen — what happens if we get caught?
**Keith**  We don't.
**POM**  But what if we do?
**Mick**  We say they're yours!
**Parry**  Go on. Ask him.
**Joe**  Well actually sir, we were wondering whether you'd like to join in this
little drinking game. It's just a bit of fun really. It's called "Beerhunter".
**POM**  "Beerhunter"? What's "Beerhunter"?
**Joe**  Well, did you ever see the film The Deerhunter?
**Parry**  You know — the Russian Roulette scene ——
**Joe**  This is a slight variation on that theme.
**Keith**  Well?
**POM**  Is it allowed?
**Joe**  Oh yes.
**POM**  Are you sure?
**Joe**  Oh yeah. It's low alcohol.
**POM**  Do I have a choice?
**Joe**  That's what I like to hear sir. Getting in the party spirit. (*To the*
*others*) Right. Ian keep an eye out.

*They prepare for "Beerhunter". Ian goes to the entrance to keep a*
*lookout. Joe and Mick clear the cake and other things from Joe's bed*
*table, and Joe pulls it up so that it is on the same diagonal as POM's*
*bed, in the middle of the acting space. Keith gets out a bandanna*
*handkerchief a small camouflage net — which is used in the same way*
*as the bandanna in the following sequence—and a pack of cards. He*

*then takes the chair by Ian's bed and puts it at the end of Joe's bed for use in the game. Parry gets out a round metal tray from Joe's bedside cabinet and puts it on Joe's table. It has eight cans of lager on it, covered with another bandanna*

**Joe**  Now then, first we all pick a card, and then there's a kind of knock-out competition.

**Mick**  Just like the film.

**Parry**  Except we're all the good guys.

**Joe**  And the winner gets the pot.

**POM**  Pot?

**Joe**  The pot. Everything.

**POM**  Oh! I thought you meant ——

**Parry**  We know what you meant.

**Mick**  What — drugs! We don't do drugs in here sir.

**Keith**  What about the medication?

**Mick**  That's completely different.

**POM**  What about the beer?

**Parry**  What about it?

**POM**  Beer's a drug.

**Parry**  No, no, no.

**Joe**  Are we playing or not? Now the winner when he wins, wins whatever we make the stakes to be, right? It could be money.

**POM**  I haven't got much left.

**Keith**  Officer in the Guards with no money!

**POM**  No.

**Parry**  Only the one stately home is it sir?

**Joe**  How did you get into the Household Division then?

**POM**  I play a lot of cricket.

**Keith**  (*after a beat*) Cricket!

**POM**  A friend of a friend — you know how it is. The Coldstream are very keen on cricket.

**Keith**  You joined the Army to play cricket?

**Mick**  But weren't you an Army Scholar?

**POM**  I only went up for an Army Scholarship because I saw a pamphlet saying they'd sponsor me through school. I wanted to stay on there, but my mother couldn't afford the fees after my parents divorced. In the end, all it meant to me was that I could go into the sixth form. I wasn't thinking about a career in the Army. I was fifteen.

*There is a stunned silence*

**Joe**  Well, I think you bowled a bouncer there sir.

**Parry** I was good at cricket you know.

**Keith**
**Joe** } (*together*) Shut up!

**Keith** Why don't we make it a dare?

**Joe** You have to abide by the final result, whatever.

**POM** As long as it's within reason.

**Joe** No sir, you can't make conditions — not when you're down here with us. Yes or no?

**POM** OK. What do I do?

**Keith** Have we got something to clean up the mess?

**POM** Mess?

**Joe** (*as Tommy Cooper*) Pick a card. Any card. There's one for you.

*They all pick cards. Keith picks an ace. POM and Ian pick high cards. Joe, Mick and Parry all pick low cards. They show their cards*

**Keith** Ace. Ace.

**Mick** Oh no not again.

**Joe** Now sir, do you want the good news or the bad news? You see in one way you've done rather well, because the higher the card the better the draw. The bad news is it wasn't quite high enough, so you still have to go into the pit.

**POM** What pit?

**Keith** It's at this point that we turn into the Viet Cong, but do it quietly lads, eh?

**POM** What pit?

**Keith** It's OK, we'll just pretend for now. Watch.

*Mick and Parry face each other across Joe's bedside table. Keith is in the middle, UC between them, and will be the MC throughout the game. The others watch closely. Mick and Parry tie the bandannas (i.e. the bandanna and net) round their foreheads, and Parry pulls his T-shirt sleeves up over his shoulders. Joe, Ian and Keith bow over the table, with their hands together as if in reverential prayer. Joe whips off the bandanna covering the cans on the tray*

**Keith** (*beckoning to Mick*) Mickeyo! (*Then to Parry*) Parryo! Lager!

*Mick and Parry wheel closer into the table, facing each other. Keith picks up a can and shows it to Parry, then to Mick, putting it right in their faces. He says something in his made-up Vietnamese, shakes the can violently and then places it back on the tray. All of this must come across like a well-practised ritual. At Keith's given signal Joe puts a hand in front of Mick's eyes and Keith puts a hand in front of Parry's:*

*this prevents them from seeing as Keith moves the beers round on the
tray, to hide the one that has been fizzed up. Keith orders Parry to take
one of the cans from the tray*

**Keith**  Dun Sa Mow, Dun Sa Mow.
**Parry**  (*doing his best Robert de Niro impression*) You want me to do
   this, huh? You really want me to do this?
**Keith**  Mao.
**Parry**  (*taking a can and holding it to his forehead*) I love you Mikey,
   I love you. (*He lets out a long defiant shout and pulls the can ring.
   Nothing happens*)
**Keith**  Dun Sa Mow.
**Mick**  I can't do it Davey. I can't do this shit man.

*Keith slaps Mick in the face*

   Fucking hell Keith! That fucking hurt. (*He rubs his face*)
**Keith**  Mao.

*Mick pulls the can ring and a plume of froth erupts from the can,
drenching him*

**Mick**  (*taking off his bandanna*) Every bastard time. It's always me first.

*In all the excitement Ian has a hyperventilating fit. The others gather
round him and help him to breathe properly again, the following dialogue
overlapping thick and fast*

**Joe**  Come on, come on. Deep breaths.
**POM**  Shall I call someone?
**Joe**  It's all right.
**Parry**  (*in his American accent*) Shake it out. Shake it out.
**Keith**  Think of something else. That's it. Think of something else.
**Parry**  Shake it out.

*There is a pause. Ian manages a laugh*

**Keith**  Ah. He's all right. Come on. It's Joe's turn. What do you think
   happens now sir?
**POM**  Let me take a wild guess. Dun Sa Mow?
**Keith**  Dun Sa Mow. Dun Sa Mow.
**Joe**  All right. Keep your hair on. (*He pulls up the chair, and ties Mick's
   bandanna round his forehead*)

*Keith takes another of the cans and goes through the same ritual. He shows it to both players, then shakes it, and places it back on the tray. Keith and Mick then put a hand over the faces of Joe and Parry to prevent them from seeing where Keith puts the fizzed-up can. Keith looks expectantly at Joe but then slaps Parry on the shoulder*

**Keith**  Kawasaki!
**Parry**  Fuck off! He's got to go first. We've always played it with the new player going first.
**Keith**  Yeah, well I'm changing it.
**Parry**  You can't, it's in the rules.
**Keith**  Oh I'm sorry Parry, I forgot that "Beerhunter"'s an official Olympic sport.
**Joe**  Oh for fuck's sake, give us it here. (*He takes a can and instantly pulls the ring but nothing happens. He laughs*)
**Keith**  (*to Parry*) Dun Sa fucking Mow you cheeky bastard.
**Parry**  OK. Joey I'm doing this for you. I'm doing this for you Joey.
**Joe**  Get on with it — you're not Robert fucking De Niro.
**Parry**  Don't say that Joey! (*He pulls the ring and is drenched*)

*The others are delighted by this*

  You rigged that.

*POM sees someone coming*

**POM**  (*hushing the others*) Oh shit! (*He goes into the corridor to keep watch*)

*They wait silently for a few seconds with POM in the corridor till the coast is clear*

  Right. It's OK.
**Parry**  That's why you wanted me to go first. You fucking rigged it.
**Mick**  How could he have rigged it?
**Parry**  You just can't handle the fact that I'm lucky. (*He takes the bandanna off*)
**Keith**  Shut up Parry and don't be such a bad loser.
**POM**  Right, I think we'd better ——
**Keith**  Now then sir, it's the moment you've been waiting for. I can see the excitement literally dripping off Mr Menzies. (*He pours beer on the already wet bandanna and passes it to POM*)

*POM unenthusiastically ties on the bandanna*

*Keith performs the same ritual as before and passes a beer to POM*

Mow. Mow.
**POM** (*doing a very bad De Niro impression*) You really want me to do this? You really want me to do this?

*They all laugh at the impression*

**Parry** That's just shit.
**POM** Remember all the trees? All the trees Nicky? I love you. (*He pulls the ring and is covered with beer*) How did I know that was going to happen? (*He bangs the can back down on the table and of course an even bigger plume of fizz gushes out, drenching him*)

*Ian then wheels himself over to the bed and POM ties the bandanna round his forehead. Ian faces Joe. The ritual continues. There are now only three cans left*

**Keith** This is it. Come on Ian. The big one. Three cans two players. Dun Sa Mow.

*Joe goes first, but nothing happens*

**Parry** Every fucking time!

*Ian picks up a can. He tries to open it. The others all take one pace backwards in anticipation but Ian can't open it. He proffers it back to Keith*

**Keith** For Christ' sake Ian. Give us it here.

*Keith carefully pulls the ring-pull. There is silence, followed by the realization that Joe is going to be drenched by the final can. He takes it*

**All** (*except Joe*) Mow.

*Joe pulls the ring; as he does so, he points the can at Keith who gets the beer in the face*

**Mick** Hey lads, lads, just think — where would we be without the Vietnam war? No "Beerhunter", hey, and no *Apocalypse Now*. (*He impersonates a famous moment from the film*) "I love the smell of napalm in the morning ... smells like ... "

*They all take a deep smell of the air*

**All**  (*except POM*) "... victory."

*During the following, Ian tears up the envelope from his birthday card and writes a word each on five separate pieces of it*

**POM**  (*drying his hair with his towel*) What happens now, a re-enactment of *A Bridge Too Far*?
**Keith**  That's good; I like that.
**Joe**  Well, when Ian wins he usually makes us have a wanking competition.
**POM**  (*laughing — then pausing*) Ian's just won.
**Parry**  Right. Well, we better get started then. Mick never does too well of course.
**POM**  You mean we're going to do it straightaway?
**Parry**  You won't stand much chance of winning if you don't.
**POM**  Look I don't think we've got enough time before dinner.
**Joe**  How long does it take you?
**Parry**  Obviously doesn't suffer from the old "premature jacky"!
**POM**  I don't think, I mean the operation. I'm not —
**Joe**  You gave your word you'd abide by the decision whatever.
**POM**  Yes, but if I'd known ...
**Joe**  You wouldn't have played?
**POM**  I didn't have much choice.
**Joe**  Sounds familiar.
**Keith**  Yup.
**Parry**  You trusted us?
**POM**  I'll know better next time.
**Joe**  You're lucky you've got a next time.

*Silence. All the men except POM put a hand down their shorts or jogging pants. POM sees this, pulls the cord of his jogging pants and puts his hand inside, reaching for his crotch*

*The others give out a whoop, as POM has fallen for the wind-up*

*During the following, Keith clears some of the cans into a black bin liner*

**POM**  Bastards! Bloody bastards!
**Ian**  Right. I know. Each one of you has to get an object from somewhere in the hospital. Last one back is a tosser and has to get some beers in. (*He hands out his notes to the others*)
**Mick**  (*looking at his note*) You're taking the piss! I can't get one of these ...

**Parry**  What's that — an erection?

**POM**  I'm terribly sorry to disturb you madam, can I?

**Ian**  No. Don't say. That's your secret military objective.

**Joe**  You'll have to use a bit of that leadership initiative then, won't you?

**POM**  I just love war games.

**Ian**  Ready?

**Keith**  Hang on. (*He puts the bin liner down by Joe's bedside cabinet and wheels the table back to its normal position at the end of Joe's bed*) Right. (*He hangs on to the back of Parry's wheelchair*)

*POM heads for the exit*

**Parry**  (*to POM*) Oi! Where are you going? He hasn't said go yet.

*They all rush at once. Parry's wheelchair bashes head on into Mick's and Keith falls on to the floor. His reaction is obvious. Parry screams out in pain and lashes out at Mick with his fists*

*Joe is frozen with panic*

**Joe**  (*after a few seconds*) Shut up!

**Mick**  What do we do?

**Joe**  (*trying to regain control*) Shut up! (*To Pom*) Get Parry back to his bay. Now!

*Parry wheels himself off followed by Mick*

**Joe**  Quick, the tins, hide the fucking tins. (*He tries to help Keith*)

*POM puts the rest of the cans in the bin liner*

**Keith**  (*shrugging Joe off*) Get off.

*POM puts the cans in a blanket from his own bed and waddles off as fast as he can*

*Ian pulls himself up and into his own bed and buries his head under a pillow. Joe cradles Keith and drags him to his bed. He stays on the bed behind Keith, holding him*

**Keith**  Jesus Joe, careful..

**Joe**  Try not to think about it.

**Keith**  How the fuck can I do that?

**Joe**  Where's the pills?

**Keith**  The pills don't work any more. Ah fuck! It's going right up. It's stabbing into my fucking bum!

**Joe**  I jest ...

**Keith**  Not now.

**Joe**  Come on.

**Keith**  Bollocks! Fucking Household Cavalry bollocks!

**Joe**  I jest ...

**Keith**  I'm frightened. Don't let them amputate it.

**Joe**  Keith.

**Keith**  I'm not going to let them take my fucking leg off.

**Joe**  I jest ...

**Keith**  No. I need to remember what this feels like. They need to know. Have you hidden the tins?

**Joe**  Yes.

*Keith screams out*

I jest. I jest.

**Keith**  Digest.

**Joe**  Teachest.

**Keith**  Beau Geste. Where are they?

**Joe**  They're coming. Chicken breast.

**Keith**  Holy vest.

**Joe**  That's a good one. Hairy chest.

**Keith**  Fucking mess.

**Joe**  Largest. (*Pronounced lar — gest*)

*Joe hits Keith in the chest to bring him round*

Come on. Largest.

**Keith**  Hard-est.

*Black-out*

# ACT II

## Scene 1

*Afternoon. Saturday*

*Keith, Joe, Ian and POM are in Bay 4. Keith is in his bed. He's had an exploratory operation on his leg. He is still suffering from the effects of the anaesthetic. The others are all confined to bed rest, and the TV is showing "Final Score". Joe is checking his pools coupon. Ian is peeling an orange, and trying to throw the peel into his fruit bowl on the table at the end of his bed. POM is standing at the end of his bed, leaning over his bedside table. After a while he walks over to the TV. He watches it for a moment, does a terrible silent fart and wafts the air in front and behind him as he walks back to his own bed*

**Joe**  That'll do nicely. Fucking bastard! Would you believe it? Sixteen points. Fucking Scarborough. They can't play football anyway. Fancy going down four-nil in front of your own crowd. (*He screws up his coupon, puts it on his cabinet and carries on with his word puzzle magazine. Then he looks up, wafting the air*) Jesus! Was that you, sir?
**POM**  (*wafting the air*) Afraid so. Sorry about that.
**Ian**  Have you got a dead rat in there?
**POM**  A whole family I should think.
**Joe**  Why don't you have another go?
**POM**  It's no good. Can't sit down. I get in there, it takes ten minutes to put paper on the seat. I managed to perch on the edge by doing this rocking motion and gripping the walls, but nothing. It's like straddling a spear. Forty minutes I was in there last time. Forty minutes!

*Ian laughs*

There's ten days' worth to come out.
**Joe**  Why don't you ask Sheila for some Fybogel? (*He turns the TV off*)
**POM**  I wish you'd call me Oliver.

*There is a silence*

What's this Fybogel then?

*Joe and Ian laugh*

**Joe**  What's Fybogel he says.
**Ian**  Laxative for elephants.
**Joe**  You take it with liquid paraffin.
**POM**  Charming.
**Joe**  Worked for me.
**Ian**  And me.
**Joe**  When the going gets tough, what do the tough do?
**Ian**  The tough take Fybogel.
**Keith**  (*sitting upright*) Pooh! What the hell's that smell?
**POM**  (*going over to Keith's bed*) Sorry Keith I've got a bit of wind.
**Keith**  I've got gangrene.
**Joe**  You haven't got gangrene. Shut up. It was Mr Menzies.
**Keith**  (*putting his arms around POM*) I love you.
**POM**  I love you too Keith. (*He smiles at Joe and Ian*)

*Keith pulls POM down on to the bed; this causes some discomfort to POM*

**Keith**  Do you want to come for a ride on my bike?
**POM**  No. Not right now Keith. Thank you. (*He heaves himself up*)
**Keith**  I'm going to bite your fucking leg off!

*Keith lunges for POM and bites his leg*

**POM**  Christ Almighty! What are you doing? Keith, get off. Ow!
**Joe**  You stupid Irish fucker! (*He breaks Keith and POM apart*)
**POM**  Shit! Shit! (*He rubs his leg with one hand and holds his bottom
    with the other*) Shit! Shit!
**Joe**  You all right?
**POM**  Yeah. He bit my leg. Shit!

*Joe puts Keith back on his bed. Keith ends up with one leg under the
sheet and the other on top*

**Keith**  Wigan 1, Doncaster Rovers 180! Brighton and Hove Albion 3,
    Queens Park Rangers late kick-off. Forfar 4, Farfor Far.
**Joe**  Shut up Keith.
**Keith**  Eh? Southampton nil 'cause they're crap. Luton departures Gate 4.
**Joe**  How long have we got this for?
**POM**  Couple of hours they said.
**Joe**  Christ!
**POM**  (*farting again*) Oh dear. Fybogel?
**Joe**  Fybogel.

**POM** (*heading for the exit*) Right.

*POM exits*

**Keith** (*looking at his leg under the sheet*) Jesus! It's gone. They've chopped it off. I never gave them permission.

**Joe** Keith! Your leg's still there. It was an exploratory operation. Look, under the sheet. Your leg's under the sheet. Under the sheet. See?

**Keith** God bless you Joe. I knew you wouldn't let them take it.

**Joe** They put a camera in to have a look. You've had a little operation Keith.

**Keith** I don't want an operation. I don't trust them. I'll get my mum and then they'll be in trouble.

**Joe** You've already had the operation for fuck's sake.

**Ian** Should we get Sheila?

**Joe** Look. One left leg, one right leg. See? They're both there.

**Keith** One left leg. One right leg. One left leg, one right leg. Oh Jesus! Where's my other one? (*He starts to get up*) I'm coming, darling.

**Joe** Oi. Where are you going?

**Keith** I've got to wash my bike.

**Joe** Get on your fucking bed.

*Joe gets up and puts Keith back to bed*

You're on bed rest Keith. You're not going anywhere. We're all confined to the bay. Do you understand?

*Mick enters*

What are you doing here?

**Mick** She's found the beers.

**Joe** What?

**Mick** Hatchet-Face has found the tins. She's called in the Colonel.

**Joe** What?

**Mick** Sheila just told me. What are we going to do? Hatchet-Face reckons there's been a breach of security. The whole place was on a bikini red the other night. We're fucked.

**Joe** Shut up. Let me think. Shit!

*There is a silence, broken by Keith with a naughty laugh. He is completely out of it*

(*Walking back to his own bed*) What did Sheila say exactly?

**Mick**  Hatchet-Face found the cans in the laundry-room. We shouldn't have done it. Not again ...

**Joe**  Right. We tell them about the surprise party — tea party and the birthday cake. And we found out from Ian that we got it wrong. But we went ahead and had the tea anyway.

**Mick**  They know we were drinking. Eh. We could say there were alcohol in the cake. Too much rum. That's not our fault. And that's what caused Keith to fall on Parry.

**Joe**  Look! The cans are circumstantial. They didn't find us in possession.

*Parry enters*

**Parry**  Hatchet-Face has found the cans.

**Joe**  I thought your mate was going to get rid of them.

**Parry**  He doesn't come round with the Naafi wagon till Monday.

**Joe**  Shit! Right — this is the story. We'd just finished tea, and you and Mick were on your way back to your bay when you heard a cry for help, so you rushed over to see what happened and Keith collapsed on your feet.

**Parry**  We could go down for this. I'm already skating on very thin ice. Having just the big toes might not get me through the medical. If I'm on a charge as well ——

**Joe**  What else do you suggest? Sorry boss, we had this piss-up the other night. I know we broke the rules but we won't do it again.

**Parry**  What about the Rupert! You don't think he's going to stick to it do you? A fucking Rupert? They look after their own. They question him he'll spill the beans, then what?

*During the following speech POM enters with a medical cup full of liquid paraffin and a beaker of Fybogel, a thick, yellow porridge-like substance*

**Joe**  Think about it. He was involved. He's not going to turn round and drop himself in it. (*Pause*) And if he did it would be us against him. (*Pause*) He's all right, he'll stick to the story.

**POM**  What story?

*Parry and Mick go back to their bay*

*Keith laughs again*

**Joe**  Shut up Keith.

**POM**  Dun Sa Mow. (*He drinks the liquid paraffin, then the Fybogel, then retches and has a glass of water*) Ach! (*He settles himself on the edge of his bed, waiting for something to happen*)

**Joe**  You wait till you've got your platoon. Playing social worker to thirty-odd guys. You'll be spending most of your time giving character references in some poxy German court or getting your head round another fucking pregnancy so that Private Toe-rag and his seventeen-year-old missis can get into some half-decent married quarters. (*Beat*) But you haven't taken that final step yet, have you? Sandhurst. That leap into the family. I hope you're learning about this family sir. (*Pause*) When you sign on that dotted line do you know what it means? Because I didn't. You're signing away your life — for Queen and Country. For Queen and Country. What is that? Those phrases, the patriotic bit, it's crap. You are in the final event prepared to give away your life. It gets worse every time I think about it — give it away for this! I ask you is it really worth it? Is it really fucking worth it?

**POM**  No one forced you, there's no conscription.

**Joe**  Don't you see that makes it even worse, because the only person I can blame is me. Are you sure you want that? Because I'm not. I'm too selfish. But is that being too selfish? They've changed me so much; my mum says they've armatized me.

*POM suddenly has to go to the toilet. It is obviously like an erupting volcano*

**POM**  Oh my God. Oh my God. (He heads for the exit) Bloody hell!

*POM exits*

*Joe is left looking at Ian*

**Joe**  What are you looking at?

*Fade to Black-out*

SCENE 2

*Early evening. Sunday*

*The Lights come up*

*Keith wheels on a payphone and sits on his bed*

**Keith**  Hiya ... Fine thanks and you? ... Good. Is she there? ... Thanks. (*Pause*) Hiya. ... Yeah, I'm fine. ... Really? Who from? Was it signed by a Colonel Stevens? ... No, it's all right I'll hold on. It doesn't take incoming calls. (*To himself*) Sly fucking bastards! (*He puts more* *money in*) Yeah, read it out. ... Ay all of it. ... Well go and get them then. (*He puts more money in*) Right, can you see it properly now? OK. Is that all of it? No, it's just a formality. Listen, you know the bit in the middle, yeah, the bit where they ask for consent of next of kin ... ay that's the bit ... well I'm instructing you to write back and say that as I'm over twenty-one you think that any decision should rest with me. ... No, just write back and tell them you don't want to override my decision. It's just a precaution you know. ... No Mummy there's no point in doing that, you can't afford to come over. I'll be home in a week or two anyway. Ay. There's the pips. ... (*Still holding plenty of change*) No. I haven't got any more; love you, love to everyone. Love you. (*He reacts as if the line has gone dead. He pauses*) What about the bike?

*Parry enters with a letter and a brown envelope*

**Parry** They're going to fail me. He's going to recommend a P8. What am I going to do?
**Keith** Don't cross that bridge till you get to it.
**Parry** I'm on the fucking bridge! I did this course once, cadre selection, just down the road at the garrison. Me and a few mates went out on the binge. It was the night before Remembrance Sunday. It was a fucking cold night. We ended up down the Embankment. You ever been down there? So many of them. In sleeping bags, boxes, bin liners. We took the piss out of them, they looked so fucking pathetic. There was this old bloke lying on the pavement. He'd pissed himself and couldn't get up. Under his coat there was a row of medals — not just long service ones but campaign decorations, ribbons. First off I thought he must have nicked them so we started winding him up but he hadn't. He'd been a Colour Sergeant with the 1st Battalion Royal Welsh Fusiliers. Fuck me! That was my lot. He had dates and stuff. Names. He knew our CO when he was still a one-pip wonder. We was all stunned. That smell. He said the Army was "his home, his marriage and his mistress"! He wanted to march in the parade on Sunday morning up at the Cenotaph, but they weren't going to let him. He'd been in trouble and they didn't want to know. You know why? He was hooked on morphine after being wounded in Korea. Thirty-odd years service and he ends up with what? (*Pause*) I am now officially eligible for a disabled car park sticker. No woman's going to want to go anywhere near me. Mick said they look like fish and chips the morning after you've thrown them in the bin. I'm never going to be a para. I always knew I'd be a para. Everything I've ever done, I've always thought "Well, it's OK. I can put up with that because one day I'll do P company and be wearing a red beret." A red beret. Stick that where it hurts, I fucking did it! Respect me then, wouldn't you?

**Keith** Apparently those disabled parking permits are like gold dust.
**Parry** (*after a beat*) Yeah, but the thing is I can't even drive!

*POM enters, dishevelled, holding a toilet roll*

**POM** I don't know why I don't camp out in that bloody toilet. Someone should have warned me about the bloody dosage. It could have been bloody dangerous. I'm dehydrating. I can't put it back in quick enough. (*He drinks a glass of water*)

*Ian enters with a letter*

**Ian** Listen. Listen to this. "Dear Ian". "Dear Ian, I am very glad to hear the good news of your improvement. I have been informed that there is now a very high likelihood of your full recovery. Naturally we are all delighted here at Battalion as of course you must be. We look forward to seeing you on your return to full regimental duties after a well-earned spot of sick leave. Regards. Colonel Nigel Colville-Dignam, CO 1st Battalion The Royal Green Jackets."
**POM** That's brilliant Ian. Well done.

*Silence. Then Parry wheels himself off*

**Keith** Parry's getting kicked out. Fuck it! Maybe there's some civvy doctor who can help me, eh? I'll have a lump sum in my pocket and a pension. Do you know what I miss? Taking the bike down on the sands, no helmet, breathing in the salty wind and flying. You open that throttle and you're flying, just clipping the edge of the sea and licking the spray, with the Walkman set to blast.

*He exits, pushing the phone trolley*

*Ian carefully folds the letter. POM watches him*

*Fade to Black-out*

SCENE 3

*Monday morning*

*The Lights come up*

*POM, Joe and Keith are on their beds. They are still all confined to the bay*

**POM** (*looking at his watch*) Twenty minutes. Still, I suppose no news is good news.

*Pause*

**Keith** (*thinking; then*) No it fucking isn't. What a stupid, ridiculous saying. No news is good news. I mean really.
**Joe** All right. Calm down. Who rattled your cage?
**Keith** Sorry.
**POM** It's OK.

*Ian enters; during the following he wheels himself over to his bed and pulls himself on to it, sitting up*

**Joe** Well?
**Ian** He didn't get anything out of me.
**Joe** Good lad. What did he ask you?
**Ian** Same as you.
**Keith** What about the cake? Did he go for it?
**Ian** Seemed to. When I started dribbling he didn't push it.
**Keith** (*to Joe*) What do you think?
**Joe** We're not in the clear yet. Five down, one to go.
**Ian** Yeah. He's called for Mick.
**Keith** Oh Christ!
**Joe** He's all right. He'll be all right. He knows exactly what he's got to do.

*Mick comes into the bay. He is walking — just, with his legs wide apart*

**Mick** The boss wants to see me next. What do I say again?

*Keith holds his head in his hands*

**Joe** It's all right. He's not going to grill you. He didn't grill any of us. It'll be a few questions. Parry was all right wasn't he?
**Mick** Yeah, yeah, but I can't last for half an hour. My mouth goes dry. I look like I've got something to hide.
**POM** Tell him you're still feeling the effects of the anaesthetic.
**Joe** That's good.
**Mick** I used to go red and pour with sweat at school when I had to go to see the headmaster.
**Joe** How the fuck did you pass your interrogation course Speedy?
**Mick** I know, I know.
**Joe** Now look! You didn't see the accident. That's all you've got to say.

**Keith**  It's simple. Your bit's easy. Now come on. All for one and one for all.

**Joe**  You were on your way back to your bay when you heard a cry for help, and you rushed over to see what happened.

**Mick**  No mention of the beers?

**POM**  Oh for fuck's sake!

**Joe**  No. It was an accident. They're looking for any excuse. Divide and rule and they've got us by the balls, but stick to the story and we're in the clear.

**Mick**  But I was thinking ——

**Joe**  Well don't.

**Mick**  What about Titania?

**Joe**  Titania?

**Mick**  The doll. We could say we filled her up with helium and she burst, and the gas went to our heads which caused the accident.

**Joe**  Please, please Mick: all I ask is to keep stum. You can still get that first stripe if you do what I'm telling you. (*He looks to POM for support*) Can't he?

**POM**  (*looking up*) Oh, definitely.

**Joe**  All for one and we're in the clear.

**Mick**  You reckon?

**Joe**  Lance-Jack by Christmas. No helium, no beer. Just go for it Speedy.

**Ian**  Show us what the Artillery's made of.

**POM**  We're all behind you Speedy.

**Keith**  You can do it Mick. We're counting on you. Go for it.

**Mick**  Yeah. You're right.

**Keith**  Course we are. We're right there with you.

*Mick moves to leave, turning in the entrance to give the boys a defiant clenched-fist gesture of support to show they can rely on him. They all return the gesture*

*Mick exits*

*The others watch him go*

We're fucked. Did you see his eyes?

**Ian**  If this gets out they're going to throw the book at us, you know that? It'll be "Squaddies in drunken accident". We'll be all over the fucking papers.

**Keith**  And if they don't get us for anything else, they'll get us on a section 69.

**Joe**  They wouldn't dare.

**Keith**  Really? Is that right? Hatchet-Face and the Colonel wouldn't dare?

**POM** What's a section 69?

**Keith** What's a ... ? (*To Joe*) Tell him.

**Joe** Conduct unbecoming.

**POM** Unbecoming what?

**Joe** Conduct unbecoming a member of Her Majesty's Armed Forces.

**Ian** Queen's Regs.

**Joe** You've heard of Catch 22. This is catch 69.

**POM** Yes, but conduct unbecoming what?

**Keith** Exactly.

**Joe** You tell me. They make the rules up as they go along. Dust on your beret. Desertion. Wearing yellow slippers.

**POM** But that's not fair.

**Joe** Who said anything about the Army being fair?

*Parry enters*

**Parry** The boss wants to see Mick.

**Joe** We know.

**Parry** Now did he tell you about the Titania idea? (*He looks at POM*) I mean if the worst comes to the worst, we could go for that.

**Joe** The worst is not going to come to the worst Parry.

**Parry** I know. I'm just trying to stay one step ahead of the bastards. Play them at their own game. Remember the drill? You fail to plan, you don't plan to fail.

**Keith** No one planned to fail Parry.

*Silence*

**POM** This is ridiculous. All over a few cans of beer! It's like being back in the fourth form again. It's so petty. There are rules. I know there have to be rules. I didn't think it was going to be ... I don't really know what I thought ... I didn't think it would be like this I suppose.

*During the following Joe meticulously sorts, tidies and rearranges the things on his bedside table. His speech is one long thought that takes him over and out of control*

**Joe** I wouldn't mind if they kept their side of the bargain, but they don't. They give you all these things to be proud of. And you don't mind giving part of yourself in exchange, 'cause that's the price. But then when you've done the job and you're the one that fell down the plughole, not your mate, they just take it all away from under you. You see it's not how good the good times are, that's easy. It's how bad the bad times get. What happens then? (*He immediately throws his bedside table and its contents across the room and lies on his bed*)

*Silence. Parry goes to pick some of the things up but a look from Keith is enough to stop him. Keith himself gets up and hobbles round the room, collecting Joe's photograph and album*

**Keith**  Pretty funny isn't it? You ending up in here with us.
**POM**  Bloody hysterical. Like children. All of us.

*Joe gets off his bed and starts to pick up his own things. He grabs the things that Keith has already picked up out of his hands. Again this is a response which is an over-reaction, but somehow, through a look or very small gesture, he tries to convey an apology to Keith. This should happen in an instant. During the following, Joe rearranges the things again and then lies on his bed*

You know in my first few weeks of university, this crusty old Colonel came to talk to all us Bursars and Cadets. He gave us a ten-minute lecture on how to avoid the undesirable elements of university life. We were not allowed to, well no, it was strongly suggested that we shouldn't mix with CND supporters, hunt saboteurs, homosexuals, and undoubtedly the most dangerous of all — sociology students. Well I turned round and put my hand up, because you see I was doing sociology. Politics and sociology. He just looked at me. Taking a mental note. You see it's just the same. Just the ——

*Mick enters*

**Parry**  What?
**Joe**  That was quick. What happened? (*He pauses*) You didn't. You fucking didn't.
**Mick**  I didn't have to. He knows.
**Keith**  What do you mean he knows?
**Mick**  He said I didn't tell them anything they didn't know already.
**Joe**  What does that mean?
**Mick**  Someone's tipped him off. I swear to God.
**Keith**  What?
**Mick**  He's got details.
**Parry**  He can't have.
**Mick**  He has. I didn't say anything.
**Joe**  Are you sure?
**Mick**  Someone's told him. The beers — everything. One of you lot has done the dirty.

*Silence*

**Parry** Well it's obvious isn't it? It's him. (*POM*) I said he'd save his own bacon. You can't trust them. It's one rule for them and one for us.
**POM** Now hold on. I said nothing to the Colonel. I'm in this up to my neck as well you know.
**Parry** Up to your waist, I should say. Makes me fucking sick. You're well out of order, *sir*!
**Joe** Shut up Parry. (*To POM*) Did you tell him?
**POM** No. I stuck to the story. I'm going to be in big trouble because of this. I wouldn't say anything. Why would I?

*Parry spits at POM and wheels himself out*

*The others look accusingly at POM*

*POM, seeing nothing but accusing eyes, gets up and exits*

**Joe** (*to Mick*) What's the Colonel doing now?
**Mick** shrugs
**Keith** Ringing all our COs probably.
**Ian** Fuck!
**Mick** I didn't even do anything in the first place.

*Pause*

**Joe** Right. I think it's time I had a little chat with the boss. Don't you? Put him in the picture. (*He gets up, stands to attention and then speaks as a Drill Sergeant*) "Detail Morgan: right turn. By the left, quick march. Left right left right left right left —" (*He heads for the exit*)
**Keith** Hold on Joe, wait. What are you going to do? Joe?

*Joe exits*

**Joe** (*from the corridor, off*) Left right left right left right left ...
**Keith** (*following Joe*) Joe! Joe!

*Black-out*

*Joe's shouting continues for a few moments; a quick burst of Tom and Jerry soundtrack comes in over this and leads into the scene change*

SCENE 4

*An hour later*

*The Lights come up*

*Ian is watching cartoons on the TV from his wheelchair while Keith is pacing up and down eating sweets. Joe enters, looking downcast. He goes straight to his cabinet*

**Keith** What did he say? (*He pauses*) What the fuck did you go and do that for? (*He sits in the big bath chair near POM's bed*) Oh shit!

*Joe takes out a couple of cans of lager. He throws one to Ian and one to Keith*

**Joe** Cheers!
**Keith** What the fuck are you doing?
**Joe** I think a celebration is in order. (*He opens one for himself and starts to drink*)
**Ian** What happened?
**Joe** Come on. There's only these left.

*Keith tries to take Ian's can from him to give it back to Joe*

**Ian** Fuck off! Get your own.
**Keith** He's flipped. Look Joe, fuck them if they can't take a joke.
**Joe** Calm down, calm down. (*As Tommy Cooper*) "I've done a deal."
**Keith** What do you mean you've done a deal?
**Joe** (*still as Tommy Cooper*) "I gave him the truth, the whole truth, and nothing but. Just like that. Ha ha." Come on Ian, you can open it.

*Ian opens his can and he and Keith get swept along by Joe's excitement and relief*

**Keith** Fuck the twenty questions Joe!
**Joe** The boss appreciated me coming forward and being so honest so much, that by the end he wasn't appreciating it anymore. Well, I did probably lay it on a bit too thick in the juicy bit. Maybe I should go into selling.
**Keith** What juicy bit?
**Joe** (*impersonating the Colonel*) "Anyway, we've decided to drop the charges and keep it in the family." The boss said "It's all going to be our little secret." Not even a sniff of a 69.
**Keith** What juicy bit?

**Joe**  Well, I thought it was only right that I told him about me and the Major's wife. (*He takes a swig*) Sorry Gill.

**Keith**  You did what?

**Ian**  What Major's wife?

**Joe**  You should have seen his face.

**Ian**  You been having it away with that Major's wife?

**Joe**  This smile of "I've really got you by the balls" just cracked.

**Ian**  She only came in for an ingrowing toenail.

**Joe**  Gritting his teeth by the end of it he was. We both agreed it could all get a bit embarrassing, you know, one way or another if it got out. Funny, not even the Major's going to know.

**Keith**  Fucking brilliant. (*He opens his can of beer*) Cheers. You fucking genius.

**Joe**  Beat them at their own game, that's what I say. Pathetic though isn't it? To save a reputation.

**Keith**  Ach! If it's going to get us off the hook you can fuck the Colonel's wife for all I care.

**Ian**  (*with real enjoyment*) Have you been fucking the Colonel's wife as well?!

*Black-out*


SCENE 5

*A few days later*

*The Lights come up*

*Keith is lying on his bed reading* The Wasp Factory

*POM is just finishing packing the last of his things into plastic bags, hoping that Keith will say something. An overnight case is packed and ready on his bed and he is fully dressed*

**POM**  Keith?

*There is a silence*

Are we going to keep this up?

*There is a silence*

Fine.

*POM gathers his case and his plastic bags and is almost out of the bay before Keith speaks*

**Keith**  So this is it then?
**POM**  Yeah. All packed. I think I've lost a bit of weight actually.
**Keith**  Oh ay.
**POM**  I just feel so much better now those stitches are out of my bum cheeks.
**Keith**  Good. Oh — do you want the book back?
**POM**  No, no, finish it. Give it back when I come and visit.
**Keith**  Right. Well mind you bring some beers if you do come eh!
**POM**  What will you do?
**Keith**  Well I'll probably have a good old cry when you've gone. No, I'll be away home in a week or two. If they ever get the paperwork sorted out.
**POM**  All this rubbish I've collected. I'm sorry to have missed the others. Say goodbye to them for me.

*POM exits, but stops in the corridor and comes back*

I'm sorry. I can't leave it like this. I've got to say something. (Beat) I didn't do it you know. I don't know how the Colonel found out, but it wasn't from me.
**Keith**  If you say so.
**POM**  Right. (*Pause*) See you.

*POM exits*

*Keith starts to read again*

*After a few moments Parry enters. He checks Pom's cabinet and under his mattress, singing "I never thought I'd miss you half as much as I do" from the Madness song "It Must Be Love"*

**Parry**  At last.
**Keith**  Why are you so chirpy?
**Parry**  The bad smell's gone.
**Keith**  Has it?
**Parry**  Yeah, and about bloody time. What was he hanging round for anyway?
**Keith**  He wanted to say goodbye.
**Parry**  I'll bet he did. Mick's off as well you know. He's got two weeks' sick leave — jammy toe-rag. It'll be you next. Where's Joe?
**Keith**  Dunno.

**Parry**  Are you still reading that?
**Keith**  Yup.
**Parry**  But it was his.

*Ian enters on crutches*

All right Ian? Bloody hell! It's Douglas Bader.
**Keith**  You can't keep a Green Jacket down can you? He'll be joining
me in pantomime this Christmas. We can both play Long John Silver.
**Ian**  (*lowering himself into a chair*) Oh fuck off you stupid Irish twat!
(*Beat*) Doesn't half make my arms ache.

*Mick enters*

**Mick**  I wondered where you'd gone. They're bringing the lunch up.
**Parry**  Lovely.
**Mick**  I'm off by the way. In case anyone's interested.
**Keith** ⎫
**Parry** ⎬ (*together*) No.
**Ian**   ⎭
**Keith**  No, seriously Mick, all the best then. Drop us a line. Tell us about
the mark two.
**Mick**  What?
**Parry**  You know, your "Go faster" stripes. (He touches Mick's crotch)
**Mick**  Get off Parry. You on heat or something?
**Parry**  Here, tell them about your holiday.
**Mick**  Yeah. Can't wait. Should be wall to wall skirt. At least that's what
they all say.
**Parry**  18 to 30 isn't it?
**Mick**  Yeah. Majorca. Should be brilliant.
**Parry**  Yeah, but what's the point — you can't shag yet, can you?
**Mick**  There's more to life than shagging, Parry.
**Keith**  Well see you then Mick. All the best.
**Ian**  All the best.

*Parry picks up and looks at the photo in the plastic frame on Joe's table,
with his back to the others and to the entrance*

*Joe enters and stands in the entrance. He is holding a rolled-up
hand towel. A brown envelope sticks out of the waistband of his track
pants*

**Parry**  (*not seeing Joe*) Don't go messing around with any big guns.
**Mick**  Ah Joe, I'm glad I caught you. I'm off. All the best then.

**Joe** Yeah, all the best.

*Parry puts the photo down and turns round. Joe goes to his bed and puts the towel on the bedside cabinet*

**Mick** I won't say good luck and all that rubbish.

**Joe** Mr Menzies gone already has he? (*He then alters the position of the photo frame very subtly, putting it back to the exact position at which he always has it*)

**Keith** He waited for you. Said to say goodbye.

**Parry** Said to say goodbye!

**Joe** That's a shame. I was hoping to have a word. Get things straight.

**Parry** Too late now. Spot of lunch Michael?

**Joe** Is it? (*Beat*) Haven't you told them your good news then Parry?

**Parry** What do you mean?

**Joe** You haven't told them.

**Mick** Told us what?

**Keith** What's going on?

**Parry** Nothing. I had a bit of good news that's all.

**Joe** That's all?

**Mick** What?

**Parry** It's no big deal.

**Joe** No big deal. What do you mean, no big deal?

**Parry** Well it isn't. Not for me. What is this?

**Mick** What's going on?

*Joe produces the brown envelope and takes a letter from it*

Oi — posted in Woolwich is it?

**Keith** Is she going to marry him?

**Parry** Have you been going through my things?

**Joe** (*reading*) "Fusilier Parry will be —— "

**Parry** (*interrupting*) Have you been going through my things?

**Joe** "Fusilier Parry will be passed fit —— "

**Parry** You can't do that. That's completely out of order.

**Joe** " — will be passed fit for clerical duties, based on his current recovery rate and no other unforeseen complications. The aforementioned P8 discharge from Her Majesty's forces will therefore be revised." Congratulations Parry. Congratulate him everybody. Was it worth it? To be a clerk?

**Parry** What?

**Mick** Worth what?

**Joe** What exactly did you and the Colonel talk about when you went in Parry? Play a bit of footsie did you?

**Parry** I don't understand. Are you actually accusing me of something?

*The lighter and more throwaway Joe is with the following, the more disturbing and unpredictable he will appear*

**Joe** I'm curious. How did you come out with it? What was the deal? Was it the clerical job in exchange for us? Just like that? Or did you have to haggle? I'm good at haggling. But I bargained from a position of strength. And I got you off the hook. But I suppose that must have thrown a spanner in the works, mustn't it?

**Parry** I didn't fucking tell him. How many more times?

**Joe** You're going red Parry.

**Parry** Look, just because they change their minds about a P8 now doesn't necessarily mean anything. That could all change tomorrow. (*Beat*) I don't want to be a clerk. I wanted to be a para. You know that.

*The others just look at Parry*

Fucking hell! Spanish Inquisition or what! (*He laughs*) This is a wind-up isn't it?

*Joe laughs*

You're trying to make me lose my rag aren't you? Like on the interrogation course. You know, to catch us off guard.

**Mick** Why should he want to catch you off guard?

**Parry** Well I don't know. Fuck you lot then. Are you going to get out of my way?

**Joe** (*maintaining that lightness*) You see something always niggled. Kept me awake. But when I worked it out I felt such a prick, because it's so obvious really. But even then I thought — no, Parry wouldn't have done that, he wouldn't have jacked on his mates. He knows what loyalty's all about. He lost his toes because he was so loyal. (*He puts his hands on the sides of Parry's wheelchair and leans into him*) Actually, he lost his toes because he was so fucking stupid.

**Parry** You've got this so wrong

**Joe** Shut up! (*He turns Parry round in his wheelchair and whispers in his ear*) On a knife edge weren't you? Admit it. Go on. (*He turns Parry slowly round again so that he is facing them all*) Be honest. It doesn't really matter now, anyway. You're still in khaki.

**Parry** I'm going now and you're not going to stop me. That bomb really fucked you. No wonder they won't let you go.

**Joe** (*lightly but with urgency*) It was the beers Parry. You gave away too much information about the beers. (*He pauses*) Now do you know where I just been? To the Naafi. To see that Corporal — you know — that friend of yours that supplies us. And you know what boys? Surprise surprise, he's been moved. Since Monday. Is there no one you wouldn't sell down the Swanee? Mr Menzies didn't know where the beers came from Parry. He didn't know, because we didn't tell him about your friend Al Capone. (*He drags the bath chair into the entrance, blocking any escape*)

**Parry** Yes he did. I remember telling him. He asked. He did. I swear.

**Joe** (*sitting in the chair*) You're making it worse for yourself Parry. We just want to know the truth.

**Parry** You're on your way out. So's Keith. Ian and Mick'll be all right. (*To Mick*) It's only going to go down as a black mark for you. Nothing serious. I've given the Army everything and they were just going to take it away from me. "Thanks very much Fusilier Parry, now sling your hook." I saw my chance and I took it. What else can I do? I don't want to be a clerk, drive a desk, but it's something. I wouldn't survive ten minutes on civvy street. I'd be homeless or in the nick. There's nothing where I'm from. Nothing. (*Beat*) They've made me. They can't just throw me on the heap. They owe me. I don't mean compensation. Five grand, great, thanks a lot. I'd rather have my toes, thanks very much. I need the life. The discipline. I need my mates. They didn't give me any choice.

**Joe** (*moving to his bedside cabinet*) Oh, there is always a choice, Parry. It's probably the only thing we have got. (*He unrolls the towel, revealing a carving knife*)

*What happens next should happen in a flash and dialogue should overlap*

**Mick** Joe!

**Joe** I borrowed this from the Naafi.

**Keith** Put it away, Joe. It isn't worth it.

**Joe** (*going for Keith with the knife*) Why isn't it? What is worth it? When does something become worth it Keith?

*Parry tries to wheel himself out. He gets as far as the bath chair but Joe catches him. Joe upends the wheelchair and, holding on to one of Parry's ankles, pulls off a slipper*

**Parry** No. Get off. Get off. Ow!

**Joe** The sentence has been passed Fusilier Parry, and will be carried out forthwith. You're to lose the big toes.

**Mick** Joe! Don't be daft.

**Joe** (*dropping Parry and going back for Mick with the knife*) You want some and all? (*He goes back to Parry and pulls him up by the feet*)

*Parry looks like a snail pulled out of his shell*

**Parry**  No. No. No. This isn't happening. Fuck you! You've got no right.
  Help me someone. Mick! Stop him for fuck's sake!
**Keith**  Stop this, Joe.
**Ian**  Joe!
**Joe**  Is there anything you wish to say, Fusilier, before the sentence is
  carried out?
**Parry**  Please, please, Joe. Stop him. I'm sorry. I'm sorry.

*Joe tries to cut Parry's toe off, but his mind hits an imaginary wall, and
he cannot go through with it. He weakens his grip on Parry's ankle;
Parry immediately pulls himself away and crawls out of Joe's vision*

*Ian throws down his crutches and buries his head in his pillow*

*Joe looks at the others. We see his distress. He falls to the floor, dropping the
knife, and howls like a wounded animal. He ends up in a foetal position*

*Black-out*


SCENE 6

*Two weeks have passed*

*The Lights come up*

*All the beds apart from Joe's have been cleared. Keith's Walkman is
on his bedside cabinet; photographs are strewn all over Joe's bed and
cabinet, with an open scrapbook and glue nearby*

*Ian is alone in Bay 4, packing his kit bag. He is wearing Army uniform
and appears to have fully recovered. During the following he pulls off
the get well cards Blutacked to the sides of his bedroom cabinet*

*POM enters. He has a plastic bag full of beers stuffed inside his zipped-up
leather jacket*

**POM**  Excuse me. Ian?

*There is a pause*

  Remember me? The Rupert!

**Ian**  Course I do, sir. All right?

**POM**  Yeah. You're looking really well.

**Ian**  Thank you sir. What you doing here?

**POM**  I'm back again. It's recurred.

**Ian**  Oh. Sorry to hear that sir.

**POM**  Not half as sorry as I am.

**Ian**  You back in the bay then?

**POM**  No. I'm in a side-room. Third on the left. (*He pauses*) You look so well. I was going to come and visit. I've been convalescing.

**Ian**  Oh right.

**POM**  (*getting out the plastic bag*) Didn't think I'd get past Hatchet-Face with these. I tried sticking them down my trousers before I came out, but I couldn't walk properly. (*He pauses*) Still, what's new? Do you want one?

**Ian**  No thank you sir. Better get on sir. Transport's waiting.

**POM**  You're off?

**Ian**  Yeah. Couple of weeks at home. Me mam's really excited. You know. Then more physio and back to the depot. All the best then sir.

*Ian puts on his beret and salutes POM*

**POM**  Yes. Indeed. All the best Ian.

*Ian exits*

*POM sits on what was his old bed. He hears the ghosts, and remembers all the things that happened to him in the bay. He sees Keith's Walkman and goes over and sits on Keith's bed to examine it*

*Joe enters in pyjamas, carrying a washbag with a towel over his shoulder. He is a changed man; this is subtle but unmistakable*

Surprise! I said I'd come back. I just saw Ian. I think he was a bit surprised too. I didn't tell Hatchet-Face because I brought these. (*He picks up the bag on the bed*) Whiff of booze and it would have been a strip search! Keith told me not to come back unless I had a few tins. Where is he, by the way? Have I missed him? I was going to come and visit. I've been convalescing.

**Joe**  Keith died on Friday afternoon. (*He pauses*) You just missed the funeral actually. (*He pours a glass of water and drinks it*)

**POM**  What?

**Joe**  They wouldn't let me go. The blood infection hasn't cleared up. They're doing more tests. They didn't have much luck with America.

**POM** What happened? He was all right when I left.
**Joe** Complications.
**POM** What do you mean complications?
**Joe** There was a blood clot, but they're not prepared to say what caused it.
**POM** But they must know. Surely someone should have detected ——
**Joe** That's all they're prepared to say.
**POM** Christ!

*There is a pause. Joe puts his washbag and towel away and starts sorting and gluing photographs into the scrap book*

**Joe** How's Sandhurst then?
**POM** I didn't go.
**Joe** I'm sorry.
**POM** Don't be.
**Joe** Given you the Spanish fiddler have they?
**POM** The what?
**Joe** The el-bow.
**POM** No. They wanted me. It's me who's given them the el-bow. (*Pause*) I just couldn't go through with it.
**Joe** What are you doing here then?
**POM** It's recurred. The pilunidal sinus. Parry was right all along. So they've got to operate again. (*Beat*) I think they're putting this one on the bill though.
**Joe** What bill?
**POM** I owe them nine thousand pounds. I've got to pay it all back you see. The scholarship. The bursary. All of it.
**Joe** Jesus!
**POM** And I haven't got a penny. My mother hit the roof. (He pauses) They're still trying to peel her off it actually. She can't help me, so I've worked out that if I can give them a fiver a week I should only be paying it back for the next thirty-four years.

*They both raise a smile*

I don't know what I'm going to do. "What to do with my life!" All that money; the Coldstream; you lot. I suppose I've been lucky in a way. I've been given a second chance. Thank you.

*There is a pause. POM gets up and puts the plastic bag full of tins of beer in the bin by the entrance on Keith's side of the bay. He stands in the entrance*

Hey, did you see that mad Scots Guard that's just come in?

**Joe** No.

**POM** He's had to come in to have his tattoos removed — he's just shown them to me. When he goes to salute (*he gestures with his hands*) he's got "Fuck off sir!" written on one wrist and "Fuck off Sergeant Major!" written on the other. Why are you in pyjamas?

**Joe** Oh, I'm part of the fucking fixtures, me! I've seen them all come and go. Even fucking Rifleman comatozed Cribbins is getting the red card before me! It's a cushy number really. (*He pauses*) Mick looked in after his holiday. Very brown he was. He's met a girl and he's thinking about a transfer to the Red Caps. He said he's fed up of big guns. Can you imagine Speedy as a copper? The terrible thing is, you can.

**POM** Well, I better get unpacked. (*He moves to the exit*) I'm in the third side-room on the left. No Majors' wives around then I take it?

**Joe** No. No Majors' wives.

**POM** (*noticing Keith's Walkman*) I don't suppose I could ...

**Joe** (*after a pause*) Go ahead. (*He moves to POM, still holding a photograph of himself*)

*POM picks up the Walkman, looks at the tape inside and smiles*

**Joe** Meatloaf?

**POM** (*smiling again*) Yeah. (*He pauses*) Hank Wangford!

**Joe** Listen, something happened just after you left ... well — look: I just want to say — I'm sorry.

**POM** What for?

**Joe** That time with the beers — I know you didn't tell the Colonel.

**POM** Did Keith know?

**Joe** Yes.

**POM** (*getting the plastic bag out of the bin*) Listen, do you want one? (*He offers Joe a beer*)

**Joe** (*thinking for a while; then*) Fuck it. Go on.

*They open the beers. Joe sits in the bath chair*

**POM** Lochaim.

**Joe** Cheers.

**POM** (*looking at the photograph in Joe's hands*) Is that you?

**Joe** Let's see. Yeah. Outside Horseguards. Buckingham Palace! The Americans used to love all that. (*As Ronald Reagan*) "You ain't seen nothing yet!"

*Joe goes over to his bed, gets a wallet of photos and goes back to POM. Because Joe has a beer in the other hand he puts the packet of photos on the floor and kneels down in front of them to find the one he wants to show POM*

What do you reckon on these then? That's the before, and that's the after. They've done some good stuff — I never did like my jawline. It's all new. The boss says there's more metal in me than the Man in the Iron Mask! And do you know where they got all the skin for my grafts? From my bum. So now I'm known as the man with two arseholes. Funny, eh? And that's Chloe. She was stunning. Really beautiful. (*He gets a photo album from the bedside cabinet and goes back to his position on the floor*) I've got another one of her — here. I was closer to her than anyone. Except Gerry. I'd sleep with her sometimes, when she was ill. She liked to have me there. I'd nuzzle my head right into her neck and she'd plant a lollopy wet one on my ear. A real softy she was. Then I'd wake up with black all down the side of my head. We used to brush them with parade gloss to bring up the shine.

**POM** Really.

**Joe** Oh yeah. Gerry was the same with Ulysses.

**POM** Who's Gerry?

**Joe** I didn't lose consciousness you see. Not until they put me under at the hospital, and that's because I panicked. (*He pauses*) The boss made a special visit yesterday. Says he thinks I should see the psycho boys — "Fuck off sir" I said. He's good like that with me — now we know where we are, none of your snob stuff. I'm not fruit and nut — but he reckons this special counselling for bomb victims might help me get over my negative attitude problem. Forgive those cunts! A legitimate fucking target, riding a horse through the park in fancy dress! I've never been to Northern Ireland. (*He pauses*) It's like when you were a kid and your dad would sneak up behind you, sweeping you up in the air out of nowhere. I could see this car. It looked like it was coming towards me. I keep seeing that Mercedes logo like a target coming towards me. They reckon the bonnet cushioned the impact of the blast. I finished up on the dash board. (*He sings the tune at the end of Cartoon Time*) You know the only thing I could think of was the wolf in "Roadrunner". His outline in the ground after falling off the mountain. "That's all, folks!" (*He pauses*) I still don't know how I got over to Gerry. They can't work out how I could even move with a compound fracture. It doesn't fit in to their rules. Mind you, I reckon if I'd seen the bone sticking out of my knee, that would have been it. He was a mess, but there wasn't any screaming. He was bent double over Ulysses. Neither of them were moving. Poor fucking animal had been severed in the middle by a car door. Gerry looked like a pin-cushion. Six-inch nails sticking out everywhere. That was a nice surprise, wasn't it? I didn't know they were nails, not until I heard the nurses in casualty. (*He pauses*) I pulled him clear. I was sure I was pulling him clear, but I looked down and his legs weren't there. That fucking car door! I held him so the nails wouldn't go deeper, but he started choking. I thought it was this nail in his cheek. I had to pull it out. I didn't know what to do. The blood was pouring out of him, oh Jesus! Suddenly the shuddering stopped and he went very still. He'd opened his eyes and he was grinning up at me, I swear, giving me that Gerry grin, and "Joe" he said, "you're the ugliest angel I've ever seen." And then he died.

*The Lights fade very slowly to Black-out*